ONLY A BOY NAMED DAVID

SHANNON SCOTT

ILLUSTRATED BY

NYA A. LUCAS

TEACH Services, Inc.
P U B L I S H I N G
www.TEACHServices.com • (800) 367-1844

World rights reserved. This book or any portion thereof may not be copied or reproduced in any form or manner whatever, except as provided by law, without the written permission of the publisher, except by a reviewer who may quote brief passages in a review.

The author assumes full responsibility for the accuracy of all facts and quotations as cited in this book. The opinions expressed in this book are the author's personal views and interpretations, and do not necessarily reflect those of the publisher.

This book is provided with the understanding that the publisher is not engaged in giving spiritual, legal, medical, or other professional advice. If authoritative advice is needed, the reader should seek the counsel of a competent professional.

Copyright © 2019 Shannon Scott
Copyright © 2019 TEACH Services, Inc.
ISBN-13: 978-1-4796-1115-7 (Paperback)
ISBN-13: 978-1-4796-1135-5 (ePub)
Library of Congress Control Number: 2019909005

The Bible and *Patriarchs and Prophets* by Ellen G. White served as references for the stories included in this book. The direct quotes by the characters, as well as the portions of the psalms, were taken from the New Living Translation. Due to the fact that it is in a journal-type format, references are noted as footnotes. If the footnote says it is based on a passage of Scripture, then the text has been paraphrased. If it simply lists the reference, then it is a direct quote.

The stories can be located in the Bible in 1 Samuel 16 through 2 Samuel 1. Although liberties were taken to elaborate on what life must have been like during David's day and what he must have been thinking or feeling, great care was taken to be culturally relevant to the time period and biblically accurate.

Scripture quotations are taken from the *Holy Bible*, New Living Translation, copyright © 1996, 2004, 2015 by Tyndale House Foundation. Used by permission of Tyndale House Publishers, Inc., Carol Stream, Illinois 60188. All rights reserved.

Published by

www.TEACHServices.com • (800) 367-1844

PROLOGUE

A DISCOVERY

He could nearly see the top of the cliff as he stretched his left hand high above his head and grasped the edge of the dry stone with his fingertips. His heart felt as if it would pound out of his chest and his legs shook so hard he worried that he might lose his footing. Ignoring the fear that threatened to throw him off the small ledge where he stood, he closed his eyes, took a deep breath, and lunged toward the sky. The leap gave him the extra inches he needed to fully grasp the high flat ledge with his right hand. At the same time, he kicked his right leg up to the side and with that momentum he managed to hoist himself up enough that he rolled over onto the flat ridge of the cliff. For a moment, he lay there, completely still, somewhat unaware of the shallow breaths he was taking. He realized soon enough, when he began coughing roughly, that he was covered in dust. Spitting and hacking, he expelled it from his mouth as he pulled himself up to a sitting position. Then he brushed it off his face.

It was then that edh-Dhib heard his father's voice. "edh-Dhib! Mohammed! Are you okay?"

He still had trouble catching his breath but after a few seconds was able to shout back to his father. "Na'am! I'm fine!"

He leaned back against the side of the cliff and tried to relax for just a bit. He probably shouldn't have been so scared about the climb, but the cliff was steep and the large boulders that he'd had to pull himself over in order to reach the cave were not close to each other. For a grown man, it was a big jump from one to the next. For a teen who hadn't hit his growth spurt, it was almost impossible. There certainly weren't any of his peers from his village who could have made it up to the cave. Smiling, edh-Dhib felt proud that his father had allowed him to make the climb.

As he began to relax, he looked out at the view in front of him. Despite the heat, a soft breeze from the sea cooled him off, and his white tunic was light and comfortable. He didn't mind the dryness of the rocks all around him because he had lived his whole life among these stones. From where he sat, he wasn't up quite high enough to see more than just the north edge of the great salt sea but the tops of the rocks all around him were some of his favorite sights. Sometimes it looked to him as if the earth ended just beyond his vision, and he often imagined that he lived in a place where he might one day be a mighty warrior who saves the earth in an epic battle.

He began to think about that, holding his arm out like he would if he had a sharp sword in his hand, when he heard a loud snort and felt something wet on the back of his neck. "Ghabi!" he shouted, turning around to look at his goat. He didn't have to guess what kind of animal had sneezed on him because he had climbed up this cliff for only one purpose—to find his mischievous and really dumb goat that had been running away all day. Frustrated, he pulled off the shemagh that he wore on his head and threw it at Ghabi. Smart enough to understand that it meant his adventures were over, Ghabi ran straight into the cave.

Throwing his head back with a groan, edh-Dhib stood up and shouted down to his father that he had found Ghabi and was going into the cave to bring him back. He picked up his shemagh, put it back on his head, and stomped into the cave.

The opening of the cave was fairly large, but as he continued farther into the space, it got a little darker and he saw that there were rocks and smaller openings all around it. He slowed down, carefully watching where he put his feet, suddenly nervous as he realized that venomous black adders often hid in places like this.

Suddenly, he heard a sound behind him, and he jumped as he felt it near him. He slowly turned and discovered a furry sakhrat hyrax, not much bigger than a cat, that lived all over the cliffs and caves nearby. Saying a quick prayer to Allah for safety and that he would be able to find Ghabi soon, edh-Dhib continued farther into the cave. He had taken about a dozen steps when he heard a familiar sneeze. He sighed and turned. There stood Ghabi looking at him while chewing and sneezing. He would have thrown his shemagh at him again except that he suddenly noticed a pile of jars next to the goat.

He walked toward Ghabi to get a closer look. The old pottery held scrolls that looked quite valuable. Something about the color of the scrolls made edh-Dihb feel immediately that these were important. But it wasn't until he picked one up and peeked inside that he saw what looked just like the Tawrat or Torah. Worried that he might damage it, he set the scroll down carefully and ran out to the edge of the cliff. "Father, come quickly! I found something!"

❋ ❋ ❋

It was 1947 when Mohammed, known to his family as edh-Dhib, found a group of scrolls as he was looking for his goat.[1] It was an extremely important discovery, and over the next ten years, researchers spent a lot of time in those caves. Eventually, scrolls were discovered in eleven caves in the area. Some of the scrolls were in jars and some were wrapped in

---

[1] British Library, "Dead Sea Scrolls," https://1ref.us/td (accessed May 28, 2019).

cloth. In fact, there are more than 800 scrolls that are now called the Dead Sea Scrolls. They are significant because they are the oldest copies of the Bible. Some of them are old enough to have been written 150 years before Jesus was born. These scrolls give us strong evidence that the Bible we read is the Word of God, written by people who lived and served Him thousands of years ago.

About 220 of the scrolls contain actual copies of the Old Testament. All the books except Esther and Nehemiah are among the scrolls. That means that almost all of the stories we love to hear about from the Bible were in the piles of scrolls found in those caves.

While the story of the Muslim teen who found the scrolls is true, we don't know if he read them. But I imagine he would have been drawn to the same kinds of stories that we enjoy, stories of courageous and inspiring people who made a difference in this world. But what if he did read them? And what if he found something extra? What if he found something that had never been seen before? What if he found a scroll with extra details about the Bible characters we enjoy reading about, like David?

Imagine if, among the scrolls, edh-Dhib found a journal written by David. What would edh-Dhib have felt as he read David's story? How would you feel if you could listen to David tell you about the amazing things he did in his lifetime? What would it teach you about courage? What would it teach you about the value of a relationship with God? What would it teach you about the battles you face in your own life?

David's story is an amazing one of courage and faith and growth, but more importantly, it is a story about a God who loves us very much. What if you were to find a scroll and when you opened it, you saw these words—"My name is David"?

CHAPTER 1

My name is David, and I am of the household of Jesse of Bethlehem. Mother gave me a scroll and an owl quill when I left some days ago to bring the sheep to the spring pastures. She told me that I will experience many days of growing and that I will gain a better understanding of Yahweh during my time here. She thought it might be good to write down what I feel and see and think. I am glad she gave me the scroll and quill because I like to write. I am also very proud because I am a good writer now. Ezra has been home from the school of the scribes for a month now and he has been teaching me to write. I am sorry that I had to leave before his return because I know I would have continued to improve if we had worked longer. But I will keep writing while I am here with the sheep, and I know that by Yahweh's blessing I will improve.

It is a large responsibility to be a shepherd. Now that I am thirteen, Father has given me the biggest responsibility of all. I will be staying with the sheep, on my own, at the spring pasture. Nethanel will come to check on me in a few days but mostly, I will be the one in charge. It will be my responsibility to watch the sheep and care for them. I alone will have to defend them against lions or bears or bandits. I am not unprepared, though. I have my small belt knife and my sling. I should probably work on my aim and speed again. One can never be too accurate when a lion is near the sheep. I will write more later.

* * *

The stars are so bright tonight. They are flickering across the sky as far as the eye can see. There are so many that I can't count them. It's quite beautiful. Not only do I see the stars, but from where I sit, all I see is sheep. They are lying all around me, and I can hear the soft sound of their breathing. I have the smallest one on my lap. I've named him Zeira, which means little one, because he is so very small. I don't know how he will ever grow but he will. In fact, this lamb should be almost as big as his father by the time we are ready to leave the pasture. But that is still a very long time from now. In fact, we will see three new moons before it is time to leave for Bethlehem.

I love the spring pasture so very much that I don't mind being here for the long, warm months. It is so beautiful. There are hills all around me so it feels at times like we are sitting in our own little valley. In many ways, it really is ours because no one comes here ... except for Nethanel who periodically checks on me. Right now the hills have almost every color I've ever seen all over them. The tall ones across the valley from me have bright flowers of yellow and purple all over their middle sections. The ones to my right are a bright green that almost sparkles when the sun hits it. Then, the ones to my left look as if an artist painted them. Sometimes I have to close my eyes and then open them again because they are so beautiful—they don't look real. Yahweh is so good. I can't believe that I get to sit and stare at this beautiful land He has made while watching the sheep.

I was so inspired by my surroundings that I wrote a song today. Well, actually, I've been working on it for about a year but when I brought the sheep back to the hillside, after they got water, I saw the sun glinting above my head and I just had to stop and stare at it because it was like nothing I had ever seen. I know Yahweh is an artist for sure.

So, my song goes like this:

> Give Yahweh glory and praise!
> His voice echoes over waters
> And His glory is like thunder.
> His voice has the power to break cedar trees
> and shake the wilderness
> He reigns as King forever![2]

I am still adjusting it to fit exactly as I want it to sound. I can hear it in my head, but I'm still working it out on my harp. It's like my sling. The only way it gets better is with practice. I was playing for Grandmother before I left, and Abinadab said I was the best musician in Bethlehem. I don't know how he can tell, but I still think I need to practice. Of course, it doesn't seem like work to practice because I love music. It just flows from me as a way to thank Yahweh for the many things He gives to me.

There is so much I see each day, and it only confirms what I know about Yahweh—He is kind and strong and artistic and merciful and powerful and just. He is so many more things. My life has not been easy. I talk as if I have lived the best life—and I have been blessed—but my life has been very difficult. I will not speak of some things because they are not my stories to tell, but my mother and I have had to live alone, and there were days as a young boy when I was very, very hungry. I know what it is to work hard and get nothing for your effort. I know what it is to be rejected and unloved. I also know what it is to see someone you love suffering. But throughout those

> *I know what it is to be rejected and unloved. I also know what it is to see someone you love suffering. But throughout those difficult times, Yahweh has always been there.*

---

[2] Based on Psalm 29.

difficult times, Yahweh has always been there. I hear His voice when I speak to Him, and I feel His presence when I pray. That is what I love so much about the spring pasture. Here it is quiet and there are no distractions. I only work and practice and care for the sheep. It is hard work but it is good work. And Yahweh is here.

✻ ✻ ✻

I finished my song today and got really quick with the sling. I have been practicing my accuracy with the release of the stone all day, and I had it down by midday when I took the sheep to water. But it was a strange day because ever since we left the spring, the sheep have been restless. I know what that means, and I have been listening and scanning the area for predators, but I haven't seen or heard any. Big predators can't hide well, so if they are here, I will see them. I don't hear any strange sounds but I do notice the sheep making strange noises. I will write again after I have checked it out.

✻ ✻ ✻

I didn't write yesterday because I couldn't hold the quill. My arm is swollen and sore from the attack that hit me about an hour after sunset. I should have known it was coming because I heard the shuffling and sort-of growling as the temperatures cooled. It wasn't dark yet when he came at them. But lions don't care about things like sunlight and warm weather. They attack any time they think they can get food. That was what he was after. Thankfully I had Zeira on my lap again because I wouldn't have been fast enough to save him if the lion had attacked on the far side of the sheep where Zeira likes to play. But the lion hit in the middle, which was to my advantage.

I heard him coming before I saw him, and I leaped into action with my sling. By the time I saw him, I was running and my arm was in full motion. I paused only for a fraction of a second to turn my shoulder toward him and then I released the stone with the fullest extension of my arm behind it. I am glad I have been practicing because the stone hit him fast and hard and right in the head. He yelped and staggered backwards, but he didn't fall. It didn't matter because as soon as I released the stone, I had another loaded and, in less than a second later, had released it in exactly the same way. The difference this time was that I was much closer. I had begun running straight toward him when I threw the first stone so when I released the second one I was only about 20 paces away from him. I could see now that he was very large and strong. He could have killed me if he had turned and pounced, but the second stone hit in exactly the right place and he went down hard. Before he could even try to move his head, I pulled the large knife from my bag and killed him.

That is why my arm hurts now. I had to put a lot of force into the knife, and with the heavy throws of the sling, it was already sore. But I didn't feel it until about an hour later. That's when everything had calmed down and the sheep were all quietly lying near me. I had been lightly strumming my harp and singing softly to calm them and to relax myself, but when I stopped, I realized that my whole right arm was swollen. It made the morning very hard. I suppose I need to perfect my ability to throw with my left arm.

Today it is much better though. I have been stretching and moving it as much as I can, even though it hurts. I know that not moving it will make it worse. Thankfully, the sheep seem to be much better today. They were kind of fearful yesterday and stayed very close to me. It's not healthy for them to be scared all the time, so I did my best to let them know that they are safe. I had to drag the dead lion over the hill to get his smell away from the sheep. When Nethanel comes, I will have to show him. My father will want to know the size of the beast so that he can keep track of the groups that hunt in this area.

※ ※ ※

Nethanel came today, and when I told him about the attack, he looked surprised. That's because the sheep seemed fine and none were missing. I don't know what he thought it was that attacked, but I walked him up the hill and stopped in front of the lion. He made a coughing and choking sound when he saw him. I had forgotten how big the lion was, but he had to have been the biggest I had ever seen. Nethanel measured his head by placing his hands over it three times and then extending his arms out to measure the body. When he stood up, he took a long breath and then spoke in a low, awed-kind of voice. "Well done, David. Father will be very proud." He put his arm around me and noticed the swelling in my shoulder. I told him it was much better and that I had been stretching so that it wouldn't get stiff. He patted me on the head and then reached into his bag. "Grandmother always knows what you might need. She sent some ointment for you." I smiled and thanked him. She does always know what I need.

※ ※ ※

This evening has been the most peaceful day since I arrived at the spring pasture. I have been using the ointment Grandmother sent, and my arm is almost totally healed. Yesterday, I sprinkled some of the lion's blood around where we stay during the evenings. I know the sheep don't like the smell, but it has prevented other predators from coming near, and as a result, we've had a very restful Shabbat. Zeira played hard today and is asleep now beside me.

Shabbat is my favorite day because things are quieter, and I spend more time thinking about Yahweh and all He does for us. We could not survive without the things He provides. It's not just the food I eat out here, but it's all the animals that live here and are able to find food. He also provides the sun and the wind and the rain and the plants and stars at night and—I could go on and on. I sang my new song to the sheep today, but as I was playing, a new song came to mind. It fits what I've been feeling this week.

> Yahweh, how majestic is your name!
> When I look at the night sky,
> I see the works of your fingers.
> The moon and the stars
> are set firmly in place
> What are we, mere mortals, that you should think about us?
> What are we, mere humans, that you should care about us?[3]

✳ ✳ ✳

I haven't had a chance to write much because it has been a busy few days since Shabbat. I am tired tonight as I sit with Zeira. I think all the sheep are tired. We don't walk around much, except to go get water, so perhaps they are tired from worry. A few days ago, the northern shepherds came through. They were from Penuel and were surprised to see me here alone with the sheep. I have never felt unprepared or unable to handle myself or the sheep, but in that moment, I wished that Nethanel was here with me.

Since these men were from Penuel, it had taken them several days to get here. They told me that they were headed further south to Hebron and were planning to sell the small herd of sheep that accompanied them. It wasn't the distance of their travel that made me uncomfortable; it was their sheep. They were scrawny and agitated. Two of them had visible sores, and they were all very quiet. Thankfully, my herd was a fair distance behind me because I had crossed the creek to speak to the men when I saw them. I must say that I wouldn't have felt comfortable with my sheep near theirs. The two men looked well-fed but the taller one was nervous and the shorter one spoke in short, vague terms. They said they had seen bandits between Gilgal and Jericho and had heard in Jerusalem that several local shepherds had lost their sheep. When I asked them why they stopped in Jerusalem, they acted strange and never really gave me a good answer.

---

[3] Based on Psalm 8.

I let them go and sent them away with blessings from Yahweh. Ever since then, I have felt uneasy.

I don't really know how to explain what made me feel uncomfortable, but I just felt that there was something not right or truthful in their story. For one thing, shepherds coming through Jericho wouldn't need to stop in Jerusalem, and they seemed so uncomfortable with the question, it made the hair stand up on the back of my neck. Jerusalem is such a big city that it would terrify the sheep. Perhaps one of them stayed out in the fields with the sheep while the other went into the city. But that doesn't explain why their sheep looked so awful. That's just bad shepherding.

Truthfully, the idea of bandits also has me nervous. I have not really been sleeping well because I feel as if something evil is around. I listen to every sound I hear around us and pray that Yahweh will protect us from whatever it is that's out there. I know He will help me—I just hope I'm ready for it.

* * *

They hit about midnight yesterday. Fortunately, I was ready. Not because of me but because Yahweh was watching over me. I had kind of dosed off around the eleventh hour with Zeira on my lap. I was sleeping lightly when I heard a sound behind me. Because I was so on edge, I jumped and whirled around all in one motion and came face to face with Mahdi, my neighbor. He is about my age, and sometimes in the spring, his father allows him to come and help me. He doesn't help much because he is not a very good shepherd, but he is fun to have around. I think his father sends him to keep him out of trouble in the city.

I excitedly whispered his name so as not to disturb the sheep but still wanting to make sure he knew how glad I was to see him. Then I noticed his face. It was white with terror, and his eyes were as large as the moon. He spoke in a short, low whisper, almost choking out the words. "David, they're up there hiding!" He pointed toward the hill to my right. I couldn't see anything, but the hairs on my body stood up. I silently grabbed him and took him behind a nearby large tree. I told him to stay behind the tree and climb it if necessary. I gave him Zeira and instructed him to take the lamb up the tree with him if needed to keep it safe.

Then I crouched down and sort of crawled to a crop of short bushes about fifteen feet away near the herd of sheep. It was very dark, but the moon shone as if right over the top of the hill, so as soon as the bandits moved, I could see them. They came creeping down over the hill, looking around them and moving cautiously. I saw four of them on the move. I couldn't tell for sure, but one or two of them looked like the guys who had come by from "Penuel." I knew we were in danger. Thinking quickly, I grabbed two sticks from the thorny bush in front of me. They had sharp, spear-like ends on them. Using both hands, I threw the sticks toward the approaching men. One landed on the right side and the other on the left. I wanted them to think they were being attacked from multiple sides.

Then I swung my sling and launched a stone at the man in the middle. I had been practicing my aim and it was spot on. It hit the man right in the chest. He cried out in pain and dropped to his knees. The way the moon was shining on them, I knew they wouldn't be able to see me well, so I continued banking on the idea that if I hit them from a variety of angles, they might believe there were more men with the sheep instead of just me and Mahdi. My only chance to save the sheep was for them to be too afraid to try and steal them. If it didn't work, I knew I would have a difficult time stopping all four of them.

I kept launching stones at them from the same spot, but I landed them perfectly on both sides so it appeared they were being fired on from different locations. Still, it was Mahdi that ended up saving the day. Apparently, the tree where I left him had a nest of biting ants at the base of its trunk. While I was firing away, the ants were launching their own attack. They had climbed up Mahdi's robe and begun biting his legs. The pain was more than Mahdi could take and he began to howl. If you knew Mahdi, you would know that he has always been a howler. No matter the type of pain he feels, he howls. It can be something small and minor or he could be losing his leg. It doesn't matter. He howls no matter the intensity of the pain. The really funny thing about him is that when he howls, it sounds like a lion screaming. It is the most terrifying sound I have ever heard. So, Mahdi began to howl and run around. Fortunately, he followed my request and he never let go of Zeira.

Between my rocks and sticks and Mahdi's screaming and running in the dark, the sheep thieves decided not to risk it. They ran back up over the hill and were gone within seconds. When Nethanel came the next day and heard the story, he said that a group of the older shepherds nearby had heard the screaming and gotten up during the night. They intercepted the men as they ran away and brought them to the magistrate the next morning. The men were so traumatized that they couldn't adequately answer questions about what they saw and heard, but they said things like a large group of fierce warriors with lions as pets were out here. Nethanel had no idea what to think so he had come out to check on me. When he heard our version of the story and saw Mahdi's swollen, ant-bitten legs, he fell over laughing so hard that tears ran down his cheeks. I would have liked Mahdi to stay longer, but he was in so much pain from the ants that he went home with Nethanel. But I had no doubt that Yahweh had sent him to save me.

※ ※ ※

When the bear came, I wasn't ready for it. I was actually feeling a little bit lonely yesterday when I thought about the fact that Mahdi and Nethanel had both gone back to the house and I wouldn't head back for many more weeks. I guess I was feeling sorry for myself. Grandmother always tells me that when we give in to thinking about ourselves the evil one jumps in and tries to pull us down. He did that with the bear. I hadn't been checking my perimeter and listening for warning sounds. I actually wasn't really watching the sheep as closely as I normally do. I'm sure if I had been I would have reacted sooner. But he came fast and hard, and before I noticed him, he'd run right into the center of the sheep fold and picked up Zeira.

If he had turned and run with Zeira, I probably would've never been able to stop him. But the bear hesitated, almost as if it was trying to decide whether it should keep Zeira or go for a larger meal. This pause gave me the opportunity to spring into action. Angry with myself for my mistake, I lunged at the bear with all my weight—and my knife. He was big, but the force of my body on his back knocked him down. He dropped Zeira and turned to attack me. I was ready, and as he swung toward me, I lunged into him with my knife. The surprise caught him off guard, and I hit him twice before he began to feel it. It made him howl in anger, but I kept at him, and with a few more thrusts, he was dead.

I didn't waste any time looking at him or celebrating. I knew I had only survived because of Yahweh's power, not my own. I immediately turned my attention to Zeira. He hadn't really moved since the bear dropped him, so I rushed over and picked him up. He was alive and breathing but clearly terrified. He had some nasty gashes in his side and on his back legs. I took him to the stream and washed his wounds. I also spooned some water into his mouth. He whimpered softly but drank it. Then I sat him on my lap and put Grandmother's ointment on his injuries. He had so many that I almost covered him with it, thankful that she had sent so much. Then I sang softly to him and the other sheep who had come to lay near me. I prayed the whole time, apologizing to Yahweh for my negligence and thanking Him for His protection.

✳ ✳ ✳

Zeira is doing much better and has been walking on his own for a few days now. That explains why I haven't written. He's kind of a naughty patient. The first few days he was sweet and calm. And he slept a lot. But as soon as he could walk, he began to get himself into trouble, heading over to the poisonous plants and roots, then near the snake holes and always to the water. I have to run after him every few minutes. But today, he got plenty of exercise and is now sleeping. As I look over the time I have been here so far, I can't believe how much has happened. Normally, when I am here in the spring, some exciting things happen, but I have never had a spring quite like this one. It's like Yahweh is preparing me for something big. I don't know what that is, but I am excited.

Yahweh is a God unlike any of the other gods that are worshiped around Bethlehem. Grandmother once told me that Yahweh is the only God who is actually real. The rest, she said, are just imaginary. They do nothing, have no power, and make no difference in anyone's lives. I know she is right when she says Yahweh cares. I have seen His protecting hand. I have also seen what He has done for my family. I know He cares for me because I feel His presence. I know He loves me. I see it in the sky and flowers and trees and water—even the sheep. All I really want is to be what He wants me to be. It's what makes me the happiest.

All of these thoughts have been flowing over me this week, and I have written a new song for Yahweh. I have seen Him work as a shepherd, especially when I wasn't a very good shepherd myself. But I'm not finished with it yet, so I will write it down another time. What I will say about it is that it's a song about my Shepherd and His goodness and faithfulness in my life.

CHAPTER 2

I am home now. But it's not really because I want to be here; I was called home. I had been adjusting to life on the pasture fine. The sheep and I had actually experienced consecutive days that were full of eating, resting, playing, and sleeping. No attacks, no predators, no problems. It was wonderful. It was the new moon, and even though I knew my family was having the new moon feast without me, I didn't care. I was enjoying my restful days with the sheep and Yahweh with no other distractions. I was thinking, talking, and singing about everything I discovered. I even finished my new song … or at least I thought I had.

But then yesterday, as I was walking the sheep back from the creek to the pasture for the evening rest, I heard Nethanel shouting at me. At first, I was confused about why he was even there. He should have been at the feast, and even if it wasn't the new moon, he never came to check on me at this time of the day. Even his behavior was strange. He never EVER shouted. As I stared at him in confusion, I realized that the only reason he might be here was because something horrible had happened at home. Forgetting about the sheep, I ran as fast as I could to where he stood.

By the time I reached him, I was panting. I asked him what was wrong. Now he was the one who looked confused. He shook his head. "It's nothing bad, David. Sorry to scare you." He paused and frowned. "But it is something urgent. And it's … confusing. The prophet has come to Bethlehem and is feasting with our father. But he refuses to allow anyone to eat until you come." I frowned at him, choking for a second on my words. Was he joking? Was he teasing? Was he serious? What could this mean? I really didn't know what to say to him in response, so I just stared at him.

"This is serious, David. The prophet of all Israel is calling for you. You'd better hurry because he's waiting. If you run, you'll have time to jump in the spring and rinse off and then change your robe before you go to the house. But if you just stand here staring at me like a confused pigeon, you'll have to meet him smelling like an ostrich." He smiled, but I wasn't in the mood to banter back and forth. The weight of the request set me into motion, and I turned and ran.

It usually takes me about eighteen minutes to run from the pasture to the house without the sheep. When I take the sheep, it is a much longer trip because they are slow. With the sheep it usually takes more than an hour to cover the same distance. But this time, I made it back to the house in just under fifteen minutes. It's not an easy run because you have to cross over two hills and the section around the trees is harder to navigate, but I was being called by the man of God, and I didn't want to meet him smelling like I did. I got to the spring just outside of town and jumped in. I dunked under the water several times and rubbed my body as best I could. I didn't think about the water dripping off me as I ran around the corner to the house. To my surprise, my sister was there and handed me a clean robe. I smiled and thanked her for anticipating what I would need. She was older than me, but we were close because she understood me the most and always seemed to know what I was thinking.

I did the best I could to shake the water out of my hair. I looked at her with a question on my face. She nodded and smiled and gave me a hug. "You look fine, David. I'm glad you washed in the spring, though." I smiled at her and then froze for a minute, unsure. "Go on, David. He's waited a long time, and the longer everyone else has to wait, the more awkward it will be. Eliab is frothing." Eliab is my oldest brother, and he is generally in a bad mood. But when he had to wait for food, he was horrible to be around. I groaned and walked to the courtyard where I knew everyone would be waiting to eat.

When I stepped out of the house, I expected to see everyone looking at me, but I guess I had taken awhile so they were all talking amongst themselves when I entered the courtyard. I was quiet, unsure of what I should do or say. The prophet noticed me instantly; his gaze was intense. Not sure what else to do, I walked up to him and bowed with respect. He tilted his head to the side as if he was listening for a bird call and then smiled. He nodded his head at me and turned to my father, "I would like to speak to your son in private." My father looked confused but said, "Of course. I have a quiet room just on the far side of the courtyard." He began to walk in the direction of the room. I waited for the prophet to move, but he pointed at me to follow, so I did. I felt the presence of the prophet behind me, but I kept my eyes fixed on the back of my father's head.

When we got to the room, my father bowed and left. Not sure what to do, I just stood there and waited reminding my confused mind that I was with the man of God. I didn't want to do anything disrespectful. Truthfully, though, I had never met him before. I had seen him when we traveled to the yearly festivals, but I didn't really know how I was even supposed to speak to him. He sat down and looked at me with a warm smile before he spoke. "David, Yahweh has spoken to me tonight concerning you." Instantly, my skin felt charged and goose bumps erupted all over my body. The prophet could see my reaction and nodded. "It is good that Yahweh's concerns are important to you. I would expect nothing less from a man that Yahweh has chosen to be His leader." I must have frowned in confusion because he smiled again as he stood. "One day, David, you will be His king." He walked toward me, and without even wondering what to do, my body and brain reacted. I dropped to my knees and bowed my head.

The prophet placed his hand gently on my shoulder and with his other hand, pulled a horn out of his belt. It was small, but as soon as he pulled it out, I knew what it contained. It smelled of myrrh and sweet cinnamon and spices—it was anointing oil. I didn't move, and I might have held my breath. He began to pour it on my head. I felt the warm oil dripping down the sides of my face and down my neck onto my back. The smell became stronger as it rolled over me. And then, I felt something I had never felt before. It was like heat and it rolled over me like a wave. It was gentle and sweet and powerful and strong and wonderful all at the same time. I knew as I felt it that it was the spirit of Yahweh. He was there and He had chosen me.

After the feast, the prophet left and headed back toward Ramah. He seemed happy and smiled at me as his donkey headed down the road. I still smelled like the oil and I still felt the presence of Yahweh surrounding me, so I went outside to be alone. I didn't want the feeling to go away—ever. Outside and away from everyone and everything going on with the feast was the best way to keep Yahweh near. It was dark, so I went out beyond the spring to the side of a hill. It was right next to the spot where I sat in the winter when I couldn't take the sheep to the other pasture. I sat and stared up at the stars and the beautiful night sky that Yahweh had made.

Just knowing He wants me is something that holds me up and reminds me that I am valuable. It means so much too, because I am happiest when I am in His presence.

As I soaked in Yahweh's presence and the beauty of all He had made, I realized that the anointing that had just occurred tonight meant something more than just the good feelings I currently had. It meant that God most definitely had a very important plan for my life. It wasn't just a feeling anymore. It was a defined awareness of Him and my future.

This doesn't mean I have any idea what His actual plan is for me, but it means I know He has something special in mind. And I, knowing and loving Him as I do, can wait until I find out what it is. Just knowing He wants me is something that holds me up and reminds me that I am valuable. It means so much too, because I am happiest when I am in His presence.

The culmination of today's events prompted me to finish my song. The words flowed so naturally as I thought about all that Yahweh had done for me and will continue to do. I was overcome by His presence, and I sang loudly and emotionally.

> The Lord is my shepherd;
> I have all that I need.
> He lets me rest in green meadows;
> He leads me besides peaceful streams.
> He renews my strength. He guides me along right paths,
> Bringing honor to His name.
> Even when I walk through the darkest valley,
> I will not be afraid, for you are close beside me.
> Your rod and your staff protect and comfort me.
> You prepare a feast for me in the presence of my enemies.
> You honor me by anointing my head with oil
> My cup overflows with blessings.
> Surely your goodness and unfailing love will pursue
> me all the days of my life,
> And I will live in the house of the Lord forever.[4]

Very soon I will be back among the sheep, happily surrounded by Yahweh's presence out in nature, but I will always cherish today's events and evening worship service on the hill.

---

[4] Psalm 23:1–6.

CHAPTER 3

It's been a while since I've written, but I'm home again and am finally taking the time to document what has been going on. I was thankful to go back to the pasture after my anointing, but as much as I would have liked to stay there forever, spring and summer came and went. Zeira is now full grown and plenty big enough to take care of himself. He thinks he is so strong and tough. He runs around and jumps and kicks to show off his strength. I laugh at him but I try not to do it loudly. He seems to take offense when I do.

My father is an important man in Bethlehem. But outside of Bethlehem, I am not sure if many would know who he is or care. The southern part of Israel is the smallest area and considered by many in the north to be beneath them. Many of them feel as if those in the south are not as intelligent, educated, wealthy, or capable. I suppose my father is considered a wealthy man since he has so many sons and livestock and grounds, but I don't know. There are several families in Bethlehem with plenty of livestock and profitable businesses, so from what I can tell, there are some who have more than us and others who have less. But I know my father feels that Yahweh has blessed him, and he works hard to live according to Yahweh's leading. I am thankful for that. There are plenty in Israel who do not worship Yahweh, which is troubling.

I am the youngest in my family, and my mother is the least of Father's wives so I am certainly no one important. But I am thankful to have a home and food. There was a time before my mother and I came to live in this home that we had no home of our own and were often without food. There were many reasons for that, some of which I don't understand, but I prefer to focus on the good things in my life right now. Being a shepherd is considered to be one of the lowest jobs, but I love it and am happy that it's my job. I know that some of my brothers would never be willing to stay with the sheep.

I have seven brothers, all of which are older than me. Their mother is Rivka, an Israelite woman whom my father married when he was younger. She runs the house and is definitely in charge of everything and everyone in it. She is not unkind to me, but neither is she nice. She's really indifferent. I think she kind of considers me like one of the servants.

My oldest brother is Eliab. He is tall, strong, and good-looking. He dresses and carries himself like the son of a wealthy man. Status is important to him, and he is very adamant that those who speak to him do so in a way that shows respect and represents his status. He is very impatient and intolerant with me. I try to stay away from him as much as I can because I can never please him. I don't try to make mistakes, but there is so much to learn about the world that I often do something he finds unacceptable. Eliab works with my father and is learning to run his businesses, so I'm sure he is just trying to run them correctly. My only real problem with Eliab is that he doesn't seem to care much about Yahweh. He never goes with my father to worship, and he makes jokes about those who do. I have even heard him refer to Yahweh in jest. It makes me angry. Yahweh is worthy of our praise and respect because He gives us so much. To hear Him spoken of in any way that is not respectful and grateful is like a slap in the face, or even worse. I can't listen to it. Eliab doesn't allow me to speak without being spoken to first so I usually just leave when he addresses Yahweh in a negative manner.

Abinadab is the next oldest, and he is kind and understanding. He knows that Eliab makes my life difficult, so he often gives me work that keeps me away from him. Abinadab also works with my father, but as the second oldest, he has to allow Eliab to lead. His temperament is good for that spot, though, because he is much more of a peacemaker than Eliab. He is sometimes hot-tempered and impatient, but he does a pretty good job of managing his emotions and controlling his words. I think Abinadab would be a great leader in the family if he were the oldest, but Yahweh knows best, and I am thankful to have him around, especially when I am near Eliab.

My older brothers Shammah and Nethanel manage the livestock. My father owns a large number of sheep and donkeys. Both Shammah and Nethanel breed and sell the animals. We also sheer the sheep and sell the wool. Ours produce a beautiful wool that brings a good profit. Shammah is precise and organized and Nethanel is thoughtful and quiet. I like working with both of them. Since I've learned how to work with the sheep, they've let me do it without too much instruction. I like the work, and they are glad to have someone who is family taking care of the sheep. Neither one of them enjoys it, and if I wasn't here, they'd have to hire a shepherd, so they treat me well.

The youngest brothers before me are Raddai, Ozem, and Ezra. Father has Raddai and Ozem managing the gardens and orchards because they are good at that. No matter the weather or pests that come, our fields are always producing and growing. Ozem works best with the trees and orchards while Raddai talks to plants in the same way that I talk to the sheep. The neighbors say their thumbs are green, but I think their entire bodies are green. It just seems they know plants so much better than anyone else. I know my father is very thankful to have them. Ezra is better inside, and before he went to scribal school, he was often in the house reading or writing. That's why my father sent him to school. It's a good profession, and even though he is gone from home a lot, he is very good at his work. My father believes that he will have a job for the king when he finishes next spring. I am always happy when he comes home because he is a good and patient teacher, and my father has given him permission to teach me how to write.

I also have two sisters—Zeruiah and Abigail. Abigail is older and falls right in between Abinadab and Shammah. Zeruiah is closer to me and falls in between Nethanel and Raddai. Both of my sisters are married. Abigail lives far away now, and we don't see her often, but Zeruiah's husband is also a southerner. They live close by, and when he travels, she stays at the house with us. She is fun and happy, and I love spending time with her. She also looks out for me and helps me avoid encounters with Eliab. He really isn't very tolerant of anyone in the household. He tolerates Abinadab the most and then it seems that it is less and less the younger we get.

Eliab has become even more intolerant of me since the festival with Samuel. He didn't witness the anointing, but I'm sure he knew something like that happened because he could smell the oil on me the minute I left the room. I tried to get out of the house as quickly as I could, but he got close enough to me to smell it. Besides that, it stayed on me for days no matter how many times I bathed. Zeruiah says he is jealous of the attention I got from the prophet. That could explain why he is so unhappy. I know from watching others that jealousy always breeds anger. In fact, I can't think of any jealous person who is happy. Eliab certainly isn't.

I know from watching others that jealousy always breeds anger. In fact, I can't think of any jealous person who is happy.

Today we all went out to help with the harvest. It's a long process that lasts several days, and everyone has to help to get it done. Eliab does the least amount of work because, as the oldest, he feels that his job is to supervise. I don't really mind as long as he stays on the other side of the field. He usually does because the workers who are hired just for the harvest never work to his satisfaction. I like working outside so I stay busy, which keeps him from yelling at me. But today, I messed up.

I had just come in from harvesting. Rivka had called us all to dinner, and my father sent us to wash because he knew she would be angry if we came to dinner without clean clothes and bodies. Most of the family went to wash in the house, but I went to the spring. It's my favorite place to wash. But I hadn't taken anything with me to dry off. I normally just run around for a while afterwards and dry that way. I knew, though, that there was no time for that. So, I decided to just sneak into the house as quickly as I could so that I didn't drip much. But in my haste, my bare feet caught the smooth stone floor and I slipped and fell. In an effort to keep from falling, I frantically grabbed at the nearest thing to me, but it didn't help.

Zeruiah heard the crash as I hit the floor and came running. I lay there for a moment in pain before I slowly sat up. When I saw her, I groaned, praying that no one else had heard me. "David, are you okay?" I nodded as she reached down to help me up. As I pulled on her to stand, she saw the fabric that I had grasped at the last second before I fell. Then she dropped me with a look of shock on her face. "David!" she gasped, "That's Eliab's new robe!" I looked down at the cloth that lay on the floor beside me and saw in horror that she was right. I would never have known except that he had paraded around in it that morning while we were all dressing for the harvest work. He had scoffed at the fact that we were all dressed in work clothes while he was dressed up to meet with a wealthy merchant from Jericho. I looked at her in panic, and then Eliab walked into the room.

"Look at the mess you've left all over the floor, David! I honestly don't know how we are related since you are always falling. That clumsiness must come from some other relation because it is nothing like the rest of us. Now you are making extra work for everyone thanks to this mess. Besides …" he stopped as his gaze took in his robe, which was on the ground next to me. Not bothering to pick it up, he grabbed my robe right above the shoulders and jerked me up so that I was level with his face. My robe was pulled tight and painfully cut into my armpits. I could barely touch the ground with my feet. As I looked at his rage-filled face, I realized that not only did my armpits hurt but my elbows, hips, and back were scraped up from my fall. I could feel a few drops of blood trickling down my left side.

"Listen to me, David." Eliab's voice was low and raspy. "Just because the prophet came and poured his oil on you does not mean that you are worth anything in this family. You will always be the illegitimate, worthless son of a lowly woman whom my father was momentarily attracted to. You will never, EVER get anything from my father's estate, and if you EVER try to assert yourself to claim any rights, I will send you out so far from here that you will never come back again!" He dropped me. "Assuming you live," he added icily.

Horrified, Zeruiah got in front of him. "Eliab, you have no right to speak to him that way. You have insulted the prophet, your father, and the entire family. It was an accident. He obviously didn't mean to fall and tear your robe!" She helped me stand again and picked up his robe. "If you were nicer, I might try and fix it for you."

He yanked the robe angrily from her hands and threw it on the ground and stepped on it. "I will not be spoken to by the daughter of an Ammonite in that way, Zeruiah. This robe is worth more than both of you, and yet I stand on it."

By that time, I was no longer scared, just angry. This was obviously my mistake even though it was an accident. If he wanted to insult me, that was fine, but he should leave my mother and Zeruiah out of it. I stepped toward him and looked up at his face with irritation. I don't know if he would have let me say anything, but I knew that speaking as he did was wrong under any circumstance, and I knew that it was right to call him on it. But just as I opened my mouth, our father walked in with Abinadab.

"What is going on here?" He looked angry and it was not just at Eliab. No one spoke for what felt like a long time. Eliab and I froze, still glaring at each other. Abinadab pulled me back, and I bowed my head to my father. He looked down and picked up the robe, pulling it from under Eliab's feet. "I see your robe is soiled, Eliab." He handed it to Zeruiah. "Will you please take his robe to Rivka, Zeruiah? Tell her I have asked that she have the servants clean it for Eliab. You can tell her that he accidentally stepped on it."

Zeruiah nodded and squeezed my hand before she left. That's when Abinadab noticed I was bleeding. "Father, David is bleeding." He grasped my arms and looked at the side of me that had hit the ground the hardest.

"Take him to his mother, Abinadab, so that she can clean his wounds." Abinadab took my good arm and pulled me out the door.

"What was that all about?" He asked as soon as we left the room. I told him the story. I didn't look up when I spoke because I had begun to feel the pain from my fall and some guilt over the whole situation. "Hmmm," he frowned. "That's not how it looked to father, I'm guessing. You might need to go talk to him. I think he's going to blame it all on Eliab."

I felt offended that I should have to cover for Eliab's insults, especially when it was an accident. I told Abinadab that Eliab had said horrible things about my mother and Zeruiah and me.

Abinadab just stared at me. "You know better, David. Eliab is rude and says things he should never be allowed to say. I'm sure Father has tried to correct that but probably not as well as he should when he was younger. But that is his own shortcoming that he will have to work out with Yahweh. It is not yours. You are responsible for your own actions." I nodded and sighed. "Let your mother fix your wounds and then find father and explain what happened."

My wounds were small and took very little time to clean. I didn't tell my mother about the confrontation with Eliab, and she didn't ask. She seemed to know that I was upset. I certainly didn't want to tell her about the rude comments Eliab had made. My mother avoided angering him just like everyone else. We had to go straight to dinner after she treated me, so I didn't get to speak to my father until after we had been dismissed. I waited until everyone else had left the room and then I went to sit near him. I think he knew I wanted to say something because he didn't get up quickly like he usually did.

I told him what had happened. My father didn't answer for some time, and when he finally did, he began with a sigh. "David, I appreciate you telling me this, but I want you to know I had surmised that exact scenario when I walked into the room. I also know that Eliab said some things to you and Zeruiah that I don't appreciate from any of my children, and certainly not my eldest." I looked at him, wondering if Zeruiah or Abinadab had spoken to him, but I didn't ask and he didn't say it. He continued.

"I know your situation with Eliab has been challenging, especially since the prophet's visit ..." He paused and looked at me. "Just understand, David, that I am very proud of you. You will always encounter people who will say things about you that are insulting and rude. But they are wrong. You are loved and valued by anyone who knows you, and Yahweh has great things in store for your life. Don't let the things said by others make you ever feel that you are anything less than chosen by God. To be chosen by Him is a great honor and He would never pick someone unworthy. That means you are deserving of all the honor He gives you."

He smiled at me and kissed my forehead as he stood. Then he walked out of the room. I had never heard him speak like that to anyone, let alone me, and I was overcome with emotion. I left the house and ran to my favorite quiet place outside so I could release what I felt. The emotions felt like the same ones that Yahweh had given me when I had been anointed only a week or so ago. It is hard to describe, but with my father, and with Yahweh, there is a longing to know that I am loved and valued. When I understand that, my heart wells up with love so strong that I know I would do anything or endure anything to honor them. So again tonight, I committed myself to honoring my father and Yahweh in all I do. It is during these types of moments that the words flow most freely in the form of a song.

> I love and praise you, Yahweh.
> Your commandments are right, bringing joy to the heart.
> Your laws are true; each one is fair.
> They are more desirable than gold!
> They are sweeter than honey!
> May the words of my mouth and
> The meditation of my heart be pleasing to you
> Because You are my rock and my redeemer.[5]

---

[5] Based on Psalm 19.

CHAPTER 4

The conversation I had with my father after Eliab's outburst helped me feel better. It's a good thing I knew he valued me because from that point on things got worse with Eliab. It was as if Eliab decided it was a problem if Father approved of me. So, he made it his personal job to verbally attack me whenever he could. For a time, he seemed to follow me everywhere I went. If I was watching the sheep, he showed up. If I walked in to eat, he blocked my path. Even when I went to bathe in the spring, I had to find a way to get there in secret or he would be there with me. It was miserable. Everyone in the household seemed to know that Eliab was bound and determined to make my life as difficult as possible.

Father was often busy and not around much, so Eliab freely abused me. I mean, he never beat me or anything like that, mostly because he knew that my brothers and Father wouldn't allow that, but his words were so sharp and painful that many times I had to run to the hills, the only place I had that was secret, to spend time with Yahweh and replace the lies that Eliab spewed at me with the truth of who Yahweh said I was. That's why the call from the palace didn't scare me as much as it did everyone else. I was thankful for the excuse to get away.

When the palace official came to our home, Father was there and Eliab was gone. I am glad, because Eliab might have beat the guy just for mentioning my name. Instead, when the man inquired to see if I could come to the palace and play for the king, Father invited him in and offered him something to eat. I was outside with Nethanel, checking the sheep for insects and any potential sores.

Abinadab came to find me. "David, you must wash and come into the house. There is a man here from the palace asking for you to come and play music for the king." Both Nethanel and I stopped working and looked up at him. Seeing my look of confusion, Abinadab laughed. "Someone obviously told them that you are a musician. C'mon, David. If you are always wondering why anyone wants you for anything, you'll never accomplish Yahweh's bidding."

I looked at him in surprise. I didn't know that Abinadab knew or cared about Yahweh's calling for me. I hadn't spoken about it to anyone. I followed him toward the house, silent and pondering. He read my thoughts. "I don't know what the prophet said to you, David, but I smelled the oil after he met with you. I also have seen a difference in you since then. Yahweh is with you, and it shows." I looked at him in surprise. He put his arm around my shoulders and squeezed it. Then he laughed. "Hopefully Yahweh isn't wanting you to serve the king all your days. I hear he's crazy." He shoved me into the spring, laughing, and I quickly washed up.

When I walked into the room where my father sat with the official, I curiously and cautiously approached. I had no idea what he would say or what was in store, but if the king was crazy as Abinadab said he was, I needed to be careful. I was hoping to get away from Eliab, but I didn't want to be around another person like him. My father spoke to me as soon as he saw me.

"David, this is Shulamith, the king's counselor and palace coordinator. The king needs a musician, and you have been recommended to go and play for him. Is that something you are willing to do?" I was shocked. I had never been asked before if I wanted to do something, especially not by my father. I simply did what was asked of me. I wondered if he really wanted me to answer. I played it safe and bowed my head with respect and told Father that if he wanted me to go, I would willingly serve the king.

My father smiled to the man. "He is an outstanding young man, and he will be sorely missed here, but we are willing to share him with the king for a few days if the king is in need of him." Father motioned for me to sit down at the table, so I did. Shulamith smiled and answered with a continued smile. It felt as if he was choosing his words carefully. "You are very generous, sir. The king is not feeling well, and the doctors feel that peaceful music will help him heal. I am not certain how long it will take, but I understand a father's need to keep his sons at home. If you have a need for him at any time, you may send someone to the palace to call for him. We are all hopeful that the king will be well in a few days."

My father nodded and turned to me. "You may go, David. Shulamith will take you to Gibeah after he finishes his meal. You may collect your things and then get yourself some food from the kitchen. Be sure to take your harp. I will speak with you before you leave."

I nodded my head and stood. Then I bowed and left, knowing that he was sending me out so they could talk further. By the time I had collected my things in a small bag and said goodbye to Mother and Zeruiah, I found Father waiting for me in the kitchen.

"I wasn't sure how long it would take you to collect your things and say goodbye so I have your food for you. I believe the man is in a hurry to get back." I nodded and thanked him for the food. "David," he looked at me earnestly, "there is something not right with the king. I am not sure what it is, but I suspect it has to do with his rejection of Yahweh. Be careful, cautious, and wise. Even though he is our king, without Yahweh, his home is a dangerous place. Spend time in prayer each day and depend heavily on Yahweh to guide you. If anything happens and you need help, send a messenger to us at once. I will call for you in a few days just to be safe." Then he hugged me. "Take care, my son. May Yahweh be with you."

I worked hard to keep my emotions in check as I said goodbye and headed north on the road out of Bethlehem. I was overcome with the words Father had spoken to me. Furthermore, besides my time in the spring and summer pastures, I had never really been away from home. I didn't expect to feel home sick, but I suddenly didn't want to leave my father. I said a short prayer to Yahweh to give me strength and help me with whatever would await me in the palace.

It was evening when we arrived so no one was around. As we entered the massive building, I looked around, trying to see as much as I could, but no candles burned, and I only saw large rooms with shadows of things that I couldn't make out. I heard sounds in the distance that I was not able to identify, but they were infrequent. I wanted to ask Shulamith but decided it might be wise to just keep my mouth shut. He led me to a room not too far from the entrance.

"This will be a perfect spot for you, David. Here you will be near the throne room where the king likes to sit. I will come find you in the morning." He smiled and looked at me, as if he was waiting for me to respond. I thanked him, and he nodded and walked out the door and then stopped. When he turned, his face looked concerned, and he wore a deep frown. "Um, it might be best if you don't come out of your room unless called for ... even if you hear noises." Then he smiled and nodded his head and left.

I tried not to be afraid as I unpacked my limited belongings, but the strangeness of his words filled my mind with wild and unrestrained thoughts, and as soon as I finished unpacking, I ran to the door and dragged a large chair across it as a barricade. I stood for a moment in panic and looked around for other things I could move. Then, as a gentle reminder, I felt the spirit of Yahweh tug at my mind, and I crossed to my bed and got down on my knees. I asked Yahweh to remove my fear and replace it with faith and trust in His leading. I asked for a heart that would share Him with the king and not be drawn into whatever evils might surround me. Then I asked Him to stay with me and give me peace. I finished with a soft song of praise, and then I laid down and went to sleep.

I don't know what time it was when I heard the noise, but I was thankful for Yahweh's presence because the racket included loud banging and loud voices shouting words I didn't understand. Within a minute, there was a knock at my door and then someone tried to open it. The chair blocked it well, and only a head was able to poke through. It was Shulamith. I quickly apologized for the chair as I got out of bed to move it. He smiled. "Actually, the chair is a good idea." The smile was quickly replaced by a look of concern. "We need you in the king's bedroom, David. Are you ready?" He looked at me anxiously. I nodded. I combed through my hair with my fingers and then picked up my harp and followed him.

We walked down a long hallway to the other side of the building, twisting and winding around many doors and turning so many times that I knew I would never find my way back to my room. We finally reached a massive door, and I heard loud grunting coming from the other side of the door. Shulamith turned and looked at me with concern but opened the door and went in. I followed, asking Yahweh to stay with me.

The room we entered was very beautiful. There was a large bed in the center, and candles were lit all around. The first person I saw was a girl. She was about my height and very pretty, a few years older than me, maybe similar in age to Zeruiah. In fact, she reminded me of her. I was so caught by her that I didn't even notice the king until I heard him groan. He was sitting on the floor in a corner of the room curled up in a ball with his arms around his legs. His eyes were closed and he groaned quietly.

Shulamith spoke to the girl. "This is David. What can we do?" She pointed at a cushion on the floor. "You can sit here. Thank you for coming, David. He's very agitated right now. I think if you play something quiet and peaceful it will help." Then she paused and looked at me with a light frown and turned to Shulamith. "He's young."

"Yes, mistress, he is, but he has been highly recommended ..." While they continued to speak, I sat on the cushion and began to strum a bit. I had asked Yahweh to help me know what to play and when to sing. I watched the king and decided to be guided by Yahweh and what I saw.

At the first sounds from my harp, the king stopped groaning, but he didn't move or open his eyes. He continued to stay in the same position. I continued to strum, and then remembered a song about peace that I had learned from Grandmother. I transitioned my strumming into that song and decided to play it first before singing. I continued to monitor the king's response to my song. He relaxed a little bit more, letting go of his legs, but his eyes still remained closed. After a few minutes, he stretched out a bit more, laying his head on a cushion that was next to him. I began to sing quietly, just the chorus to start. He seemed to calm down more, so I stopped looking at him and just focused on the music. I sang the long version of the entire song.

I must have closed my eyes when I sang because I didn't see the king move from his spot on the floor. As I finished singing, I kept strumming because I wasn't sure how much more music he needed. Looking around, I saw that the king was now lying in his bed. Shulamith was lying by the door and looked to be sleeping. The girl was next to me, watching the king. When I looked at her, she didn't move but spoke in a low voice. "Sing one more, David. I want to make sure he is fully calm before you stop."

I sang another song of peace and praise to Yahweh, and when I finished that one, she thanked me and told me that the king was sleeping so I could stop. We all left the room, and she told Shulamith to get me some breakfast from the kitchen. "I think David should come to the throne room this afternoon. That's when he usually begins to lose his mind and wellness. The stress of the court in the morning seems to bring it on." Shulamith nodded and began to walk away. As I followed, she reached out and touched my shoulder. "Thank you, David. You are a very good musician, and you made him calmer than he has been in a long time." I smiled and bowed and then followed Shulamith.

I found out from listening to Shulamith and the kitchen staff gossiping that the girl was the daughter of the king. Her name was Michal, and she was his youngest daughter. King Saul had four sons and two daughters. His youngest son was about my age, but his others were quite a bit older with the oldest near in age to Eliab. I also learned from listening that the king had been acting crazy for a few months now and all the palace staff were convinced he was possessed by a demon. He screamed and grunted and shouted in a deep voice with words that no one understood. He sometimes thrashed around and threw things and ran himself into walls. It had gotten much worse in the last few weeks and all were hoping that peaceful music would help him.

When Shulamith took me back to my room, he told me that he didn't think the king was possessed, just guilty. He said he knew the king was feeling the results of his rejection of Yahweh but just didn't know what to do about it. "Sing him more songs of Yahweh and His forgiveness this afternoon, David. Maybe that's what he needs to hear the most." I nodded and spent some time in my room talking to Yahweh and thinking about the songs I could sing for the king.

That afternoon when I entered the throne room, I felt tiny and doubtful. It was so big and overwhelming that it seemed as if my voice and little harp would not even be heard. The king sat on his throne with a frown on his face, but he looked much more like a king than he did during the night. His counselors stood behind him talking quietly with each other, and the scribes sat on the side of the throne working at tables. I looked at Shulamith, and he nodded to start. Again, I strummed softly at first, playing the music before singing. As I had done before, I stopped worrying about the king and what was happening around me and I just focused on the music and the worship of Yahweh.

I sang three songs, and when I finished the last one, I felt very tired, as if I had been running or climbing. I looked around and saw that the counselors and scribes were now gone. Shulamith was sitting with his back against a wall and his eyes closed. The king was still on his throne. There was another man in the room sitting on the floor next to the king. The king spoke and the man stood up and moved to the king's side. "Come here so I can speak with you, zammar," he called to me.

I stood up and walked in front of the king and bowed. "What is your name, young man?"

I told him and he smiled. "You are a very good musician, David, and very young for a zammar. Are you trained?"

I lifted my face carefully before I informed him that I had not received any formal training, just instruction from my family.

"They have trained you well," he said. "They are all singers and musicians?"

I shared that it was my grandmother who taught me. Although my father and one of my brothers are musical, they don't practice because they are too busy farming.

The king smiled when I finished sharing about my family. He then turned to the man beside him. "Make sure you pay the zammar well, Jonathan."

They did pay me well, which was a blessing. I spent a few days there before my father came to get me. Despite the beauty of the palace and the compliments I got, I didn't like being stuck in the palace, so I was so thankful to go home. I preferred the sheep and the pasture to the king's court and the palace. After I said hello to my family, I went straight outside to be with Zeira and sit in the pasture where I could have a nice long talk with Yahweh without interruption.

The king continued to need my music and would call for me every few weeks. It seemed that the music soothed him for a few weeks at a time, and then he would start to be bothered again. Each time I went, I felt more comfortable because the palace staff knew me and welcomed me. I didn't need Shulamith to lead me around anymore. I could easily find my way to the king's room if he needed me at night. He seemed to be doing better, though, and usually only needed me in the throne room after his court time. Sometimes he asked me to sing for meals or events, and I did a variety of songs depending on what kind of setting it was. I sang lighthearted songs for festive events and peaceful songs when the king needed to rest. The one constant is that I always sang of Yahweh because I agreed with Shulamith that Yahweh was the king's greatest need. I liked the king, and as I got to know his family, especially Jonathan and Michal, I wanted for the king to be well and for him to reconnect with Yahweh. I knew from my own life that a connection with Yahweh was the only thing that brought joy and peace in life. I knew without a doubt that the king needed that too.

CHAPTER 5

Time has passed quickly since I wrote last. Grandmother always called the passage of time, the nature of time. She meant that it was how time worked. There is nothing we can do to make it move any slower or faster. Time has passed her as well. Not too long after I got home from my fifth trip to the palace, she fell asleep and never woke up. She had a peaceful look on her face, and I know she rests, waiting for Yahweh to wake her. But I still miss her very much.

Time is moving me along too—I have just moved into my fifteenth year. I feel exactly the same as I did a year and a half ago when I began to chronicle my experiences in the pasture, but I know I am different. Probably even more different than Zeira who is now the biggest sheep in our flock. For one thing, I look different. I am much taller and stronger than I was. I am also quite skilled and confident with the sling. Some days I spend hours practicing. Nethanel calls it my deadly weapon because I have been using it effectively on the lions and bears that continue to come at the sheep.

About two weeks ago, a lion tried to attack the herd in the middle of the day. When I struck it with the sling, it screeched, but then it turned on me. It was the biggest one we've had this year, and as it lunged toward me, I instinctively grabbed the sides of its head and threw it down on a large boulder. It died on impact. I know Yahweh guided me in that moment because I would've never thought to go after a lion barehanded. This and other instances have caused my faith to grow, along with my strength. Looking back on this instance and others, I can see how Yahweh was preparing me for a dangerous adversary much bigger than a bear or lion.

We are currently at war with the Philistines. They had been attacking the countryside north of us, all the way up past Gibeah and the king has called for a strong offensive against them. He wanted more than just the militia, and a message went out to every village asking for the help of all able-bodied men, not too young and not too old. I wanted to go but Father said I was needed here. He sent Eliab, Abinadab, and Shammah. They had been camped in the Elah Valley for more than 30 days. Father hadn't said much about the war so I assumed it was because there was no news. But late last night he called me to him before I went to bed.

When I entered his study, I could tell he was worried. "David, I have heard nothing from the battlefield. I only know they've been camped at Elah now for too long, and I am worried. Your mother made some food for them." He handed me a bag. "Please take this roasted grain and bread. I am sure they are not eating well. And here …" he handed me a second bag. "Take this cheese to their unit commander. Find out how they are doing." He grabbed my shoulders and looked me in the eye. "Please bring me back some news that they are okay. They are fighting the Philistines, you know." I nodded and he kissed my forehead. "Thank you, David. May Yahweh bless your journey."

I left very early the next morning because I wanted to make it there before mid-day. Nethanel said he could manage the sheep with my nephews. They needed something to keep them out of trouble anyway. I was excited to travel because the distance is not too far, and I love being outside. I had my harp and sling with me—my two prized possessions. With all my encounters while sheep herding, I have learned to keep my sling tied to me so that I can use it quickly. I can release the stone now as fast as I can move my arm.

The weather was fine, and I moved quickly. As I drew near to the camp, I could hear the war cry. I walked up the back of the hill where they were stationed and saw the army taking battle formations along the top ridge of the hill. I ran to a young boy who was helping the last soldiers replace supplies. I asked him to watch my bags. He looked at me proudly. "Yes, sir!" I smiled and thanked him and gave him a handful of the cooked grain. Then I ran up to the front lines where the soldiers had lined up. I asked the first soldier I came to if he knew where the sons of Jesse of Bethlehem were stationed. He pointed about a dozen men down the row. I ran to them and wrapped my arms around the back of Abinadab. "Father will be so happy that you are okay!" I hugged Shammah and even Eliab, although he just stood there and looked at me.

Before I could say or ask anything else, I heard shouting and pounding from across the valley where the Philistines stood. I turned and saw the most enormous man I had ever seen. He was a giant. Even his shield-bearer was taller than any man in the army, and this man was at least a foot above that. By my view, he had to be about nine feet tall. His armor, which matched his size, was obviously bigger than anything I had ever seen. Carrying it would probably be like picking up a large boulder. His spear was so thick it outsized some of the tree trunks dotting the hillside. I was captivated. That's when I noticed the terror in the faces of the Israelite soldiers. Then he spoke.

"Why are you all coming out to fight? I am the Philistine champion, but you are only the servants of Saul. Choose one man to come down here and fight me! If he kills me, then we will be your slaves. But if I kill him, you will be our slaves! I defy the armies of Israel today! Send me a man who will fight me!"[6] He continued to hurl insults and vial words at our soldiers. I could feel my heart racing. I was so angry. With each slur, I felt my pulse rising. I decided that as soon as the soldiers charged,

---

[6] 1 Samuel 17:8–10.

I would go with them. I waited for just a second, sure we would surge forward at any second. But no one moved. I turned with my fists clenched and looked at face after face. Everyone registered outright fear. Our soldiers were afraid of him! I was so shocked that I froze and stared at the man next to me.

I guess he could tell that I was surprised because he began defending himself and all the other soldiers for that matter. "Did you see that giant? He comes out every day to defy Israel. He is terrifying! He is such a champion fighter that no one is willing to face him. We know we will all die and become their slaves. The king doesn't know what to do. He has said that he will reward anyone who can kill the giant. He has promised great riches, his daughter, and tax exemption. But the man is so intimidating that no one is willing to do it! I sure don't think it's worth the risk."

A wiser man would probably have kept his mouth shut, but I was so offended by the things the giant was saying that I began talking—rather loudly. I was raging on about how this giant shouldn't be allowed to insult our nation, king, and God like that, so I didn't notice my brother storming up to me.

"David!" He shouted at me in anger. His words were vicious. "Why are you here? You are such an irresponsible child. Who's watching the sheep? Are you wasting away our family's livelihood just so you can come watch a fight? I know how you are. You are lazy and arrogant. You always think you're so good, so tough, so big. You are nothing, David. You should be at home. Go back to the sheep and leave the fighting to us men!"

If I had been at home, I might not have responded to him at all. I was used to his jealous words and rude comments, but for some reason today I couldn't shake off the anger I had toward the irreverent Philistine, and I turned it on my brother. I told him to back off because I hadn't done anything wrong. I told him no one else had been brave enough to fight. This infuriated Eliab, but my last comment pushed him over the edge. I asked him why he hadn't gone out to fight him.

Eliab and I were in each other's faces, pushing with our chests against each other. Neither one of us wanted to back down. He wasn't much taller than me anymore, and I wasn't about to let him have this one. We might have come to blows except that I suddenly felt someone grab my back and pull me. Then I heard a familiar voice. "David?!" It was Shulamith. He walked up to me, passing the large soldier who had pulled me away from Eliab and put his hand on my shoulder. "Are you the one who has been yelling at the giant?!" He almost laughed, but the soldier next to me nodded his head and pointed. Shulamith looked at me as if he was trying to figure out a riddle. "The king would like to talk to you." Eliab threw up his arms in frustration and shook his head as I followed Shulamith toward the king's tent.

When I walked into the king's tent, I could tell he was struggling. He had that sort of crazy look on his face that he would get before I sang for him. Jonathan stood near him and his other sons were on the other side of the tent. There was also a combination of scribes and counselors, in addition to General Abner nearby. I didn't know for sure why he wanted me, but I realized I had left my harp with the boy and would probably have to go get it. "Here he is, my king." Shulamith bowed and I bowed my head.

"David the zammar is the one talking about fighting the giant? My singer?" It took me a minute to realize that he had called me because someone repeated to him what I had said to the soldiers. I began to feel a sense of excitement inside me that I couldn't fully explain, but I didn't need to. Before I could think, words poured forth in earnestness. I confidently told him that no one needed to be afraid of this Philistine. I told him I was his servant and that I would go fight the giant. King Saul seemed to grasp my emotion, but still he shook his head. "David, you can't go fight him. You are just a boy! He's their champion! He's a seasoned warrior. He's been fighting since he was your age!" He shook his head again. "No, no." But something in his voice gave me a sense that he might budge, so I pushed back.

I said these exact words. "I have been taking care of my father's sheep and goats. When a lion or a bear comes to steal a lamb from the flock, I go after it with a club and rescue the lamb from its mouth. If the animal turns on me, I catch it by the jaw and club it to death. I have done this to both lions and bears, and I'll do it to this pagan Philistine, too, for he has defied the armies of the living God!"⁷ Every person in the tent was listening to me now, especially the king. "The LORD who rescued me from the claws of the lion and the bear will rescue me from this Philistine."⁸ I meant every word of what I said. I was not afraid to fight the giant. I knew Yahweh was with me and would win the battle for me.

I could see on the king's face that he believed it too. At least somewhat. After a long pause, he said, "Go. May Yahweh be with you." Then he stepped down from his throne and began to put his armor and large helmet on me. The problem was that Saul was almost a giant himself. When I stood next to him, I only came to his chest. He is the largest man in Israel. So his armor dragged all over the ground when I tried to move. I told him it was impossible for me to walk in the armor, so I began to take it off. Some of those within the tent began to protest that I couldn't possibly fight without it. I moved quickly. I don't know if they thought I was giving up or if I had decided to go look for other armor, but I didn't waste time explaining. I just bowed to the king and ran out of the tent.

> *"The LORD who rescued me from the claws of the lion and the bear will rescue me from this Philistine." I meant every word of what I said. I was not afraid to fight the giant. I knew Yahweh was with me and would win the battle for me.*

I had seen a creek at the bottom of the hill near the valley, so I ran around the king's tent and jogged down the hill. I only had my staff and my sling, which I always kept strapped to my arm. I knew I would need stones. I was thankful there was a great selection of them by the creek, and I chose five smooth, round stones with a nice hefty weight. I put

---

⁷ 1 Samuel 17:34–36.
⁸ 1 Samuel 17:37.

four of them into my pouch and then began to walk toward the center of the valley.

I was already about ten strides across when the giant noticed me coming. I don't think his eyes were very good because he got excited when he first saw me and picked up his spear. His shield-bearer walked in front of him. They almost pranced as they walked out toward me. I am sure they thought I was the mightiest of all the soldiers in Israel. I can say that because when they got closer to me, close enough to see me better, they froze. I thought they would laugh because I was only wearing my short robe that I had traveled in and nothing else. But when he spoke, I could tell he was insulted.

"Am I a dog that you come at me with a stick?"[9] He also said some vile curses that I would never write down. But they sure made me angry. "Come over here, and I'll give your flesh to the birds and wild animals!"[10] I stopped moving and just looked at him and a feeling of fire came over me. I felt as if I would explode. There was more rage within me than I had ever felt for Eliab or anyone else who insulted me. I know it's because of his words against Yahweh. I wasn't even hearing what he said about me. I only heard his insults to God.

This was my response to him. I never want to forget the exact words I said. "You come to me with sword, spear, and javelin, but I come to you in the name of the LORD of Heaven's Armies—the God of the armies of Israel, whom you have defied. Today the LORD will conquer you, and I will kill you and cut off your head. And then I will give the dead bodies of your men to the birds and wild animals, and the whole world will know that there is a God in Israel! And everyone assembled here will know that the LORD rescues his people, but not with sword and spear. This is the LORD's battle, and he will give you to us!"[11]

My words filled him with rage. In anger, the giant pushed up his helmet, exposing his face and, I noticed quickly, his head. The rest happened

---

[9] 1 Samuel 17:43.
[10] 1 Samuel 17:44.
[11] 1 Samuel 17:45–47.

so fast, but I will never forget any moment of it. After lifting his helmet, he ran toward me. I ran at him, keeping my eye on his face and that of his shield-bearer who was now behind him. Waiting for just a second longer than I did with the lions and bears, I slipped the stone into the sling with one motion and then flung my arm forward with all my might. I didn't wait to see if the stone hit its target. I knew it would, so I just kept running.

When the stone hit, it hit so hard that the sound echoed across the valley. It seemed as if everything slowed down. I could see that it broke into his forehead, and while he tried to keep moving, his body stopped working. He continued to try to run as he tipped forward, but at the same time, he grabbed his face in reaction to the pain in his head. In less than a second, he fell straight down to the earth. It sounded as if a tree had fallen because the ground shook beneath him.

I reached him just after he fell. I doubted that he had died from the stone, although he was badly injured. But neither of those things was relevant because his entire army stood behind him and his shield-bearer, another giant man, was only a few steps behind. I knew I had no time to contemplate, so as soon as I reached him, I grabbed his sword from his hands. It was so heavy, I had to use both of my hands to lift it, but I did. Then I brought it down with all my might on his neck.

I am quite sure that every person who watched me walk across the valley was sure that Goliath would win and that Israel would be defeated. I certainly know that Eliab was sure of it. But when they saw me lift the giant's head into the air, they roared and charged. The shield-bearer had frozen when he saw me with the sword. Now he turned and ran in the other direction. The army of Yahweh chased them all the way to Gath and Ekron.

Today was an incredible day. I am lying in a tent documenting all that happened. The giant's sword is next to me on the ground, longer than I am tall, and the tired soldiers around me are sleeping peacefully. I am happy not just because we won but because Yahweh won. This was His victory, and it was important because His own people have lost confidence in Him and His ability to win these battles. If just one of them, even my brothers, had believed that Yahweh could win this war, they would never have hesitated to fight the giant. I know it was not my ability that won this battle. It was Yahweh's. It doesn't mean that I won't continue to practice with my sling, because I know that Yahweh uses our abilities. But no matter how good I get as a fighter, I will win only when I fight for Him. Anything I do, I must do for Him. That is what brings me joy. In fact, I'm working on another song.

> I praise You, Lord, with all my heart;
> I tell everyone about the wonderful things You have done.
> I am filled with joy because of who You are.
> I sing praises to your name, Most High.[12]

---

[12] Based on Psalm 9.

CHAPTER 6

I am a prisoner in the palace. I'm not actually in the prison, so I guess it could be argued that I am not actually a prisoner. But I am not allowed to go home or see my family, and I am struggling with that. It really happened after the battle with the Philistines. When I killed Goliath, I was so happy for my people. I was thankful I could help the king and my brothers. It seemed like nothing bad could come again. That is obviously not the case, but I was very excited—all seemed right with the world. None of the things that have happened since then were things I would ever have been able to imagine, but each one is the result of that battle. Some of the things that have happened to me have been wonderful, and I am so thankful for them. But some of the things have made my life even more difficult than it was before.

It started with General Abner. After the battle was won, I came back to the hill and found the boy with my things. He was very excited and seemed impressed with me, which was kind of different. But I thanked him and gave him some of the bread and cheese. Then I took the rest of the items my father had sent and gave them to my brothers and their unit commander. I was saying goodbye and getting ready to leave for home when the general came to the tent. He told me that the king was looking for me. I figured he just wanted to say thanks or something, so I said goodbye to my brothers, grabbed my things and followed the general to see the king. It was my intent to leave from there for home.

When I got into the tent, the king asked me the strangest question. "Whose son are you, my boy?" I told him Jesse from Bethlehem was my father. I thought he already knew that since I had told him that before when I played music at the palace. Well, as soon as the words left my mouth, he began to give commands, and things started happening. In just a few minutes, I realized what was going on. He sent someone to my father's house to let him know that I would be staying with him indefinitely! He didn't even consider if I wanted to do that or not. I started to protest because I really just wanted to go home. But Shulamith stopped me. "You cannot decline this, David. He is the king, and he is not asking you. You have no choice in this. To go against the king's order would be to risk your own life and that of everyone you love. He is taking you as his possession and is now sending someone to notify your father." He continued after seeing the shocked look on my face. "I know this isn't something you want, but Yahweh sees and knows. He must have something in store for you in this as well."

I didn't know what to say, but I decided to follow Shulamith's advice and not push back against it. Thankfully, Yahweh did have something in mind to help me get through this, and I am hoping that someday I will understand how this too has been part of His plan for me. But right now, I am struggling, even with the blessings He has sent.

One of those blessings has been the king's family. I met Jonathan for the first time when I played for the king in his throne room. But when we went back to the palace, I saw him often. He has become my closest friend. I think he understands that his father makes my life difficult at times, and he does his best to try and counter it. As the oldest son in his household, he is the next in line for the throne. There are many in Israel who hope this will happen because Jonathan is well loved and a very good man. He would be a just and fair king. But that time is not yet in Yahweh's plan because King Saul still rules. I must be careful with how I write this. I would never want to cause any problems for Jonathan because he is like a brother to me.

A few days ago when I was feeling trapped and confined in the palace, I snuck out at night so that I wouldn't go crazy and do something that would get me in trouble. I suppose that sneaking out could get me in trouble, but I had been watching and the night guards were careless and lazy. That's not a good thing for the safety of the king, but it has been helpful to me. I could see that if I timed it right, I could climb out a window and they would never see me. As long as I came back at the right time, I would be able to do this without discovery. It would give me some of the time I desperately missed with Yahweh and not risk anything for me or my family. So, I began sneaking out.

When I got out of the palace, I would head into the hills to a tree I loved. I had seen it in my travels to and from home. Near the tree was a spring and some beautiful flat areas where I could sing and talk to Yahweh without being heard. On my second escape, I went out to this secret place and just lay there quietly for a long time. It had been a tough week at the palace because the king was feeling so worried about something. So, he had ordered me to stay with him all the time. I couldn't leave his side for any reason. I even had to sleep on the floor in his room. I was exhausted, so when I escaped the palace and got to my spot, I just lay on the ground outside, soaking in the earth. Then I heard someone walking in my direction. I had nowhere to go, so I froze and lay as still as possible, hoping they wouldn't see me. As the figure approached me, I could tell it was Jonathan.

I still didn't move because I knew I wasn't supposed to be outside the palace, and even though he was always nice to me, he was the king's son. I didn't think he saw me because he walked around the other side of the tree and had his back to me the whole time. He sat quietly against the other side of the tree for a long time and then spoke. "This is my favorite place to come, too, David." I tried not to jump even though my heart was racing faster than I thought possible. Since I had been discovered, though,

I got up and told him that I just needed to be outside sometimes where I can hear Yahweh's voice better. He nodded and said, "I know. I heard you singing to Him the last time you came out here."

I tried not to look panicked, but I was. I hoped the dark would be able to hide it. I asked him if he was going to take me back to the palace. It was the question that concerned me the most. If I got in trouble, I could handle that better than if I couldn't come outside again. "No," he smiled. "I am here to join you. Is that okay, or would you prefer to be alone?" I told him I would enjoy his company.

We spent several hours there talking and enjoying the peacefulness. We began meeting up on a regular basis. We couldn't get out every night, but when one of us needed the opportunity to escape, we had a secret way of communicating that to each other, and we would meet there during the night. Some nights we would talk. Other nights we explored. Sometimes, we sparred. Jonathan was an excellent fighter, and I had only ever learned to throw my sling and take down predators. I had a lot to learn about fighting the kinds of battles that soldiers and princes fought. He was a good teacher, and I learned quickly. These escapes and the time I've spent with Jonathan have helped me get through my imprisonment the most. Without him and our time together, I would not have been able to endure. I miss my family and my home so very much. Even worse, I don't know when I will see them again. As long as the king stays in his current state, I don't think he will ever let me go. I asked Jonathan about it on one of our visits.

Jonathan looked thoughtfully at me for a while before he answered. "My father believes that the kingdom and, actually, he himself, is more secure if he has a connection with someone that is favored by Yahweh. Ever since your victory over Goliath, he has kept you with him because he feels that you are the only reason we win our battles. In his mind, you are his protection." I was shocked. Did he really think that? It was incredulous to me that he wouldn't directly connect with Yahweh himself. He didn't need me to do that! "I know what you're thinking, David, but my father doesn't want to connect with Yahweh. He has convinced himself that

Yahweh won't allow that, even though we tell him otherwise. Even the high priest has told him. He just won't listen. He feels he will only receive anything from Yahweh because of you." He sighed. "I know you miss your family, David. I have tried very hard since the beginning to talk my father into allowing you to go home. I'm sorry that I haven't succeeded."

His words terrified me in so many ways. I was afraid at the thought that even Jonathan had no power with his father. I was also afraid that I might never see my family again. But I was even more afraid that the king had so rejected Yahweh that he couldn't be convinced that Yahweh desperately wanted a relationship with him. I shuddered at the idea.

A few days later Jonathan and I met again at the tree. I was expecting to practice sword fighting. I had gotten pretty good at it and wanted to show him. Instead, he wanted to make a covenant. I was confused and asked him why we needed a covenant.

"We're like brothers, David. I love you like my real brothers, and it's important that you understand that. It is obvious that Yahweh honors you and has chosen you for something great. Perhaps you will even be king someday. I want you to know that even though Saul is my father, I am loyal only to Yahweh. If he chooses you, I will follow." I felt uncomfortable. I believed that Jonathan would be an excellent king. Yahweh certainly felt the same way. I was sure of it. I stepped back from him.

> *I want you to know that even though Saul is my father, I am loyal only to Yahweh. If he chooses you, I will follow."*

"David, do not resist what Yahweh ordains. It's true that we don't know the future, but He has directed you to this point, and He will continue to do so. I know you want to do what He calls you to do. So do I." Then he took off his robe and put it over me, along with his armor, his sword, his bow, and even his belt. He knelt down and made a covenant of loyalty to Yahweh and me as Yahweh's king.

As I write this, thinking back to that moment, I am overcome with emotion over Jonathan's loyalty and commitment. I still don't fully understand why Jonathan made a covenant with me. The only way I can wrap my mind around this is because Jonathan loves Yahweh and wants to serve Him. That is something I understand. Yahweh means more to me than anyone or anything. Even more than my family. Jonathan feels the same way. We both know that Yahweh is worthy of that kind of respect and love. Because Jonathan understands those feelings, it has helped me to better manage the fear I have about my future. I am afraid that Yahweh might actually want me to be king someday. I am afraid at what that would mean for Jonathan or my family. Not knowing the future is so very hard. But Jonathan's faith in Yahweh gives me courage, and I trust that Yahweh will make it right. All of these thoughts and emotions have flowed out into a new song.

> I will exalt You, my God and King.
> I will praise Your name forever and always.
> I will praise You every day.
> Great are you Lord and worthy of praise![13]

---

[13] Based on Psalm 145.

CHAPTER 7

I am quite sure that Jonathan didn't say anything to his father about our covenant, and I am also quite sure that no one else witnessed it or knew that it had happened because, in the king's mind, it would have been treason. As time moved on, King Saul astonished me by putting me in charge of the soldiers. I suppose in part it was related to the fact that we won every battle I entered. But I know it was because of Yahweh that we won. I was grateful for Jonathan's instruction in the art of fighting, but it is foolish to think that my newfound skills had anything to do with our victories. I know without a doubt that Yahweh gave us the victories. Regardless of the reason, while the soldiers liked me and were pleased when I led, it brought on a whole new set of problems.

For one thing, General Abner was now a fierce enemy. He had been tolerant of me before, but now he hated me. He made my life very difficult. With my new job as leader of the soldiers, I dealt with him every day. But despite his attempts to cause me to fail, the soldiers improved, and we continued to win. Yahweh gave me wisdom, and I encouraged the men to fight as loyal representatives of His people. I turned their attention back to Yahweh, which gave them a purpose and meaning. They began to feel that they were capable of great things. Their renewed confidence in Yahweh was what helped us win our battles. I loved this group of men, and I felt honored to join them in battle.

Things changed for us, however, when we were returning from another victory over the Philistines. It was customary that when the armies returned home from a victory, the townspeople would congregate along the sides of the road leading up to the palace and cheer. The soldiers looked forward to this, and excitement always grew as we approached town. This time I knew there would be trouble as soon as I heard the cheers. The women sang the loudest, playing tambourines and other musical instruments while they danced. "Saul has killed his thousands, but David has killed his tens of thousands!" I didn't bother looking at the king because I felt his hatred as soon as he heard it. I certainly didn't look or smile at any of the women. I prayed they would suddenly become unable to sing. I would have preferred if they had switched up our names and sang that I had only killed a thousand. But they just sang louder. By the time we reached the palace, the king was seething.

I heard his voice after he slammed the door to his room. "They've credited David with tens of thousands, but only credited me with thousands. What's next for him—the kingdom itself?" I wanted to melt into the floor. How could I possibly help him if he thought I was trying to take the kingdom from him? I was very upset. I didn't know what to do to make things right. It would do no good to talk to Jonathan because he had seen the whole thing. I also couldn't tell Shulamith because he had no authority over the king. I had only one option and that was Yahweh. I spent the night in prayer, putting my problem before God. In the morning, I felt much better.

The king, however, was worse. It was as if a demon had entered him. Perhaps jealousy is like a demon, for I certainly know that the evil one plays a part in jealousy. But whatever it was, it was worse than the madness I had been originally called to the palace for. He walked around mad and angry, garbling his words and foaming at the mouth sometimes. He would have fits of rage, exploding at anyone who might only mildly disagree with him. Sometimes he would lay despondent and consume himself with self-loathing. Other times, he was just mad.

He still seemed to enjoy hearing my music so I spent much less time with the soldiers and much more time playing for him. It seemed to help. He calmed some when I played, and I began to do it daily. Then yesterday, while I played for him in the afternoon, things took a turn for the worse.

He had been out of sorts the previous day, so Jonathan had canceled the morning court and let the king sleep in late. However, he woke exhausted. I played softly for him while he ate and then continued as he sat and rested. I began to sing softly of Yahweh's goodness. I used the gentlest voice I could on his favorite song. Seconds later, I felt a whir of wind go by me. I instinctively rolled to my side away from it. When I looked where the wind had been, I saw the king's sword. He had throne it at me, and it had pierced the wall

"He is afraid of you," he said. *"He sees that Yahweh is with you and not with him. He cannot win against you and doesn't know what to do."*

with its force. I froze in horror at the sight because it hung right over where I had been sitting. I knew without a doubt that the whir of wind that had pushed me to the side was the presence of Yahweh. He had saved me. I ran out of the room, coughing in terror.

Jonathan found me a few minutes later and checked to make sure I was fine. He said his father felt horrible about it and didn't know what had come over him. After resting for a bit, I went back to play again in the evening. I tried to ignore the earlier event. As I sang the praises of Yahweh again, I felt a deep calm and sense of peace about my life. But the king was clearly still very angry with me and it bothered me.

Shulamith came to my room later that evening. "He is afraid of you," he said. "He sees that Yahweh is with you and not with him. He cannot win against you and doesn't know what to do." I fumed in anger and fear. I didn't understand how the king couldn't see the fact that I had served him faithfully and had never given him any cause to think that I wanted to steal the throne. Shulamith read my thoughts. "The king knows that you are loyal to him, but he also knows that you serve Yahweh above all. That and the power that Yahweh gives you is what scares him the most."

I didn't know what would happen, but I was thankful when the king chose to put me back outside with the army. He had allowed General Abner to be in charge again, which improved my relationship with the general, but he did give me my own unit, which was exactly what I needed. I was allowed to work with my men on my own and train them as I pleased. Abner felt that it was a group not worth his time, so he left me alone as well. As a result, we worked together well, and because Yahweh was always with us, we were continuously victorious.

Saul continued to be uncomfortable around me, and it didn't help that the people of Israel continued to praise my victories. I told them every time they did that it was only due to the work of Yahweh. I wanted to make sure all the people knew that with Yahweh all things are possible and without Him nothing is possible. I wanted them to know that everything I did that was good was because of His work. Some listened, for which I am thankful, but they still cheered loudly when I was victorious, which angered Saul even more.

I struggle with trusting Yahweh to handle my problems each day because I feel that I have so many. I look around at all my enemies and wonder if I'll ever escape. Most days, I just wish I could go back to watching sheep and fighting lions. It was so easy. But I know that Yahweh needs me in this place. Even though I can't understand why, I want to do whatever He asks of me. So, as always when I struggle with doubt and fear, or anything else, He gives me a song, and it makes me feel more connected to Him.

> How great is the goodness You have stored up
> for those who fear You.
> You lavish it on those who come to you for protection,
> Blessing them before the watching world.
> You hide them in the shelter of Your presence,
> Safe from those who conspire against them.
> You shelter them in your presence,
> Far from accusing tongues.
> Praise the Lord, for He has shown me the wonders
> of His unfailing love.
> He kept me safe when my city was under attack.[14]

---

[14] Psalm 31:19–21.

CHAPTER 8

Despite my time outside and my continued victories, the king refuses to see me as someone who supports him. He sees me only as a threat. It makes things uncomfortable for me, and he doesn't benefit from my music very much anymore. I enjoy the time outside that I get to spend with Jonathan, though. Because he is the crown prince, he is even above the general in his leadership of the army. They all love him, and we enjoy the fighting games and challenges that we use for training.

I began to notice some months ago that the king's daughter, Michal, was always coming outside to watch the training. She is not like her sister who prefers to stay inside and despises all things related to warfare. She is also very pretty, and I have found myself distracted sometimes when she is outside watching us. I nearly lost a limb once because I was looking at her instead of at my right side. Fortunately, the soldier who was training with me missed my arm by a fraction of an inch. I learned my lesson that day.

Not too long after, though, I was able to see her without the risk of death from an errant sword. I had gone into the palace to get some food, intending to go back outside since I was not yet cleaned. I chatted briefly with the cook and then headed back out. I almost knocked her over when I exited the kitchen because she was entering at the same time I was leaving. She appeared embarrassed, and it almost seemed as if she had been standing outside the kitchen listening. But I shrugged the idea away because I couldn't imagine that she would have any reason to do that. Yet she spoke to me a while, and despite my hurry to get back outside, I stayed. Every time I believed the conversation was over, she started another topic she wanted to discuss. It confused me.

    I asked Shulamith that evening if he had noticed any change in her. He burst out laughing at my question, which annoyed me. I wasn't trying to be funny. I was just confused. "Are you that unaware, David?" He laughed again. "Michal is in love with you! Everyone knows it." I was horrified. It's not that there wasn't a thought of joy at the idea that a pretty princess might love me—it's just that this was the daughter of the king who hated me! I could barely talk or move without fear that he might kill me. What could possibly be good about thinking that his daughter was in love with me? I must have looked as terrified as I felt because Shulamith laughed again. "She won't kill you." I frowned and shot back that it wasn't her that I was worried about.

    I don't know if the king knew how his daughter felt or not, but he had clearly been getting some comments about the fact that he had promised to give his daughter to the man who killed Goliath. He called me in to see him a few days later. "David," he spoke immediately when I walked into the room, "I will give you my oldest daughter, Merab, in marriage on this condition: you must be my warrior and fight all the battles for Yahweh." He smiled, but it looked very forced. I hesitated, wondering what he was trying to do. I honestly didn't need or want a wife, and I certainly had no interest in marrying Merab. I'm sure she felt the same. But I couldn't shake the advice that Shulamith had given to me when the king took me to be his possession. I spoke carefully. "I am not worthy and neither is anyone in my family to become a relative of the king." He must have agreed because sometime later, he gave Merab away in marriage to someone from Meholah.

I wondered about the conversation because it seemed as if the king didn't really want me to marry his daughter. I finally asked Jonathan why he even offered it. He sighed, which was a usual occurrence when he spoke about his father. "I am sure he is trying to trap you, David. He believes that since he can't harm you, he can maybe pass you off to the Philistines. If he sends you to them and you die, then he is not to blame." I frowned. It was a horrible thing to hear. Jonathan saw my face and reminded me. "David, no one has control over my father except the evil one. I have tried to talk him out of his madness, but he even shuts me out. But remember, Yahweh is with you. Nothing my father does and nothing the Philistines do can harm you when you serve Him." I knew he was right, but I struggled to keep the fear at bay.

I was thankful for that conversation because not too many days later the king tried again. This time he sent his servants to me to tell me that he liked me and wanted me to be his son-in-law. I looked at them with my arms crossed, and they understood that I didn't believe them at all. So they left. But they came back to me the next day and gave me a challenge from the king. If I killed 100 Philistines, then I could marry Michal. I asked for time to consider it, and then I prayed. If it was Yahweh's battle, then I would let Him lead it. Whatever came from it would be to His glory. So, I agreed, and I spent the season fighting the Philistines. When I returned, victorious, the king had to keep his side of the bargain.

He did. Michal and I were married that month, and once it became official, I was very happy about it. Michal was funny and strong and not afraid of her father. There were times when it seemed like she could have fought the wars right along with us, but she was much prettier than any of the soldiers. She reminded me in many ways of my sister Zeruiah because she was always joking and loved to tease. Of course, I teased her right back. Our running joke had to do with the fact that she had spied on me in the kitchen that first day we talked. Each time I would accuse her of spying on me or having loved me first, she would give me a reason why she had not. We always laughed because we knew we had both loved each other from the first day we had been together in the king's room. I was so thankful to Yahweh for her companionship. It made the difficult times much easier to handle.

Our marriage didn't help the king like me more, though. Only a few days after our wedding, Jonathan came by to tell me that the king had ordered my death. Michal and I were horrified. I was his son-in-law, after all. Jonathan looked tired, but he told me that I shouldn't worry. He had been able to talk to the king and remind him of how much I had done for him and for Israel. He recounted to him the many times I had saved the lives of his people and that he could never kill the one who Yahweh had sent to save us from our enemies. Jonathan's defense had worked, and the king had promised to him that as the Lord lived he would not kill me.

We went to war again shortly after that, and it was a dominant victory for our army. I again reminded the men to give the glory to Yahweh, but the people began to talk openly about me, saying that I had wisdom and heroics. I prayed about it, hoping that the king would not be angry with me. That night, however, when he called me in to play and sing for him, he threw his spear at me just as he had before. Again, the presence of Yahweh moved me from his aim, and I ran out and went home.

Only a few days after our wedding, Jonathan came by to tell me that the king had ordered my death.

That same night Michal came home terrified. She had been in the palace just before and had heard her father telling his most trusted soldiers to come by our house the next morning and kill me. I couldn't believe it. Again?! I didn't know if it was real or not or if he would change his mind. I struggled to know what to do. The last thing I wanted was to leave my house and Michal. But I also didn't want to die. She insisted that I leave. She believed that her father was serious about his threat. Tying fabric together, she made a rope that hung from the window of the house to the ground. What a marvel she is. I kissed her goodbye and slid to the ground. I knew exactly where I was going to go.

I don't know what happened the next morning, but before I left she told me her plan. She was going to stuff pillow and clothes under the covers of the bed to make it look like I was sleeping. She would insist that I was sick and not to be bothered. I knew that if it worked it would only be for a short time. Both of our lives were in danger. She insisted that she would be fine. She said her father might be angry but that he would never kill her. I was doubtful, but I put it before Yahweh and went to Ramah as soon as I was away from Gibeah. I had to see the prophet.

I had tried to avoid seeing Samuel as much as possible during my time at the palace because I did not want the king to attack him. Still, he was the only one who I knew was strongly connected to Yahweh, and I needed his wisdom right now. Every time I had gotten the opportunity to talk to him, it had helped tremendously.

It didn't take long for the king to find out where I was. The next morning a group of messengers showed up at Samuel's place where he instructed a group of prophets. The messengers asked for me. The prophet didn't even open the door. He actually acted as if there was nothing he needed to do. He allowed Yahweh to handle it all. So, when the men walked up to the door, they suddenly stopped and began prophesying and praising Yahweh right in front of us! It was so amazing to see that I stood at the window despite my fear of death.

Saul heard about the failed attempt and sent another group of messengers to take me out and kill me. They stopped in the same exact place as the others and did the same exact thing! This happened three times! Not once did Samuel ever worry. Finally, the king himself came to Ramah. This time, I was genuinely afraid. Still, Samuel's confidence was so strong that I allowed myself the chance to watch the king as he walked up. When he reached the same spot where the others had been overtaken with prophesying, he stopped. He, too, was overcome and fell down on the ground and prophesied and praised Yahweh! I couldn't believe it! The terrifying, demonic king laid down with no power at all because of the presence of Yahweh. He stayed there all day and night before Samuel picked him up and sent him home.

He had been humiliated by this event because many people had come to see the great king lying on the ground prophesying. So, as he left, he promised me that he was at peace with me. I appreciated the gesture, but I didn't believe his words any longer. I spent the evening with Samuel and Yahweh. The prophet's trust in Him was so strong. I want to have that kind of confidence. I try, but I struggle when things get tough. My constant prayer during this time at Samuel's house has been that I would better trust Yahweh and submit to His leading in my life.

> You are my strength; I wait for you to rescue me,
> for you, O God, are my fortress.
> In his unfailing love, my God will stand with me.
> He will let me look down in triumph on all my enemies.
> But as for me, I will sing about your power.
> Each morning I will sing with joy about your unfailing love.
> For you have been my refuge,
> a place of safety when I am in distress.
> O my Strength, to you I sing praises,
> for you, O God, are my refuge,
> the God who shows me unfailing love.[15]

---

[15] Psalm 59:9, 10, 16, 17.

CHAPTER 9

I felt restored and refreshed from my time with Samuel, and I was confident that Yahweh would watch over me. But I was not confident in the king. I knew I had to figure out a way to be sure that things would be safe for me, or I might never be allowed to see Michal again. I had to talk to Jonathan. I found him, but in the presence of my best friend, I was overcome by emotion.

I cried out to Jonathan and asked him what I had done to wrong his father that he would want me dead. Jonathan assured me that, although his father was mad and acted without reason, he would never go that far. "No, David! My father would not do that. Listen, he doesn't make big decisions without telling me first. He wouldn't hide something like this from me!" I shook my head. I told Jonathan that his father wasn't stupid. He knew we were like brothers, so he would naturally keep something like this from Jonathan so as not to upset him. I told him I was sure I was close to death.

We decided to put this theory to a test. The next day was the new moon feast, and we both knew that the king expected us to be at the dinner party as a sign of loyalty to him. Of course, I had no intention of going because I was sure he would use the opportunity to kill me. So, we made a plan that I would go visit my family in Bethlehem. This was a blessing to me in itself because I hadn't seen my family in so long. Jonathan would attend the festival at the palace and watch his father. If the king didn't get angry about the fact that I was with my family, then I would know that it was safe to return. If he reacted, then we would know his threats to kill me were real. I was to meet Jonathan in a field near the palace in three days. He would come with his arrows and a boy to catch them. If he told the boy that the arrow was on his side, then I would know it was safe to come back to the palace. But if he told the boy that the arrow was past him, then I would know I had to leave.

I went home, happy to see my family, but my heart was heavy because I truly believed that the outcome wasn't going to be good. I spent a wonderful time with my family during the feast, and I prayed and sang and celebrated. Yet the heaviness of my mind was obvious, and my father asked to speak with me before I left. He didn't waste any time. "Are you in danger, David?" I tried to keep my spirits high, but I looked defeated and admitted that that was what I feared. I explained to him what was happening with Jonathan and what I would find out when I met him. I knew that danger to me also meant danger to them, so we put a plan together to keep them safe should it come to that. Then we prayed together, and he hugged me and gave me his normal blessing. I left with a mix of sadness and happiness.

When I arrived at the field, I didn't have to wait long for Jonathan to show up. I could see the boy and the arrows he threw. I anxiously waited to hear his words. It felt as if my heart was going to beat out of my chest. I heard the boy shuffling around and then Jonathan's voice pierced the air, although it sounded as if it would break. "The arrow is past you, my boy! Hurry!" He said it with urgency. A flood of emotions immediately overcame me. I was thankful the boy left quickly. When I heard the silence, I came out, weeping. Jonathan dropped down beside me. He, too, was sobbing. He bowed before me and hugged me. I didn't know if I would ever see him again, and my heart broke.

When we finally parted ways, it occurred to me that I was not only a fugitive, but I had no place to go. It was a terrifying thought. I had gone from being son-in-law to the king to a homeless wanderer with a death warrant. I quickly lost the confidence I had spent so much time building with Samuel. I decided then to go to Nob. Ahimelech, the high priest, was a kind and generous man, and I thought he could help me.

When I came to his door, he seemed surprised and afraid. "Why are you alone, David? Why is no one with you?" He looked around me to try and make sense of it. I knew he was a wise man, and if I hadn't been so panicked myself, I perhaps would have realized that he suspected correctly what had happened. But I was too afraid and desperate, and I made a mistake that makes me sick now to describe. I lied. I told him that the king had given me secret orders to carry out. I told him that my troops were meeting me at a secret location. I then asked him for some food.

He looked around and said he had nothing except the holy bread, but he could give that to me if my men were not impure. I assured him that they were pure, and then I asked him if he had a spear or a sword because I'd had to leave in a hurry and didn't have time to get mine. "The sword of Goliath is here. If you want to take it for yourself, then take it because it's the only one we have here." I was glad to get it because it was a great weapon. I asked him to get it for me.

When we finally parted ways, it occurred to me that I was not only a fugitive, but I had no place to go.

As I waited, I noticed a man sitting quietly at the side of the room. He seemed not to be paying attention to any of the conversation. In fact, he seemed not to even notice me. But when I looked at him a second longer, I realized who he was, which made me very uncomfortable. I had intended to stay there with the priests because it felt like the safest place, but this man was Doeg, the king's chief shepherd. He was an Edomite and one of the meanest people I had ever known. He held the position of shepherd for the king, but all who spent time at the palace knew him as a mercenary. I didn't want to be anywhere near him.

My fear was all encompassing in that moment. Looking back on it now, as I write, I realize that lying was such a big mistake. Time will tell as to the repercussions of my actions. I just know that I wished I had trusted Yahweh more. I don't feel at peace right now, because I let go of my commitment to always let Him lead, and I chose to lead myself. I don't know what the future holds, and I'm scared.

CHAPTER 10

I left Nob, trying to think of a place I could go where I would be safe. The only place I knew of that Saul would never bother to look was in Philistia. So, I decided to go there. I am still amazed that I even considered this to be an option because I had just spent the last few years killing Philistines and I was forever known in that land as the man who killed Goliath. I guess I thought maybe that they didn't know all the things I had done and probably couldn't pick me out easily since I had always fought in war against them. Who spends their time remembering faces when a war is being fought? I underestimated my fame.

Gath was the closest of the Philistine cities, and I had heard that King Achish was a reasonable man. Besides, I had never seen him before, so I could probably sell myself as a fighter. They were always needing those, and if I could keep myself hidden from the ones that might possibly recognize me, I should be able to establish my value enough so that it wouldn't matter who I was. I did just that.

I approached the garrison near the city gate. A short and stocky servant opened the door and asked me to wait while he went to get Achish. He asked who I was, so I told him some of my accomplishments and that

I was looking to join the ranks of Achish's soldiers. It seemed like a good idea at the time. The short and stocky man seemed to be no one I thought would know me. But another servant helping him was very tall and strong. Something about him made me uncomfortable, so I looked down at my shoes for a few minutes and then shrugged it off.

When Achish appeared, he began to interview me. I tried to stay out of the view of the tall servant, but Achish kept asking him questions. All of a sudden, the tall servant looked at me with surprise. "Seren Achish, isn't that David, prince of Israel? He's the one that people sing about." He began to sing and dance, hopping around on his feet like a child and very off-key. It would have been funny except that the song he sang was: "Saul has killed his thousands, but David has killed his tens of thousands!" When he finished dancing, he made sure that Achish understood that those tens of thousands were Philistines.

My plan was quickly backfiring on me. I panicked! Terrified and unsure of how to get out of this, knowing that I would surely be dead in a few minutes if I didn't do something, I did the only thing that made sense at the time—I acted like a crazy man. I knew exactly what that looked like from my time with Saul.

I began to drool and let the spit dribble down my chin. I shook my head around and bobbed up and down like a bird in mating season. I even copied the little dance that the tall man had been doing, laughing and grunting to myself. To make it even better, I scratched the walls of the buildings and the gates of the city, jumping up and down with squeaky sounds in my voice.

Achish had seen enough. "Can't you see he's crazy?" he yelled in the face of the short servant. "Why did you bring him to me? Am I short on insane people that you bring one to me so he can go crazy right in front of me? Do you really think I want him in my house?" He stomped into the building and slammed the door. I ran around in circles for a minute longer and then bolted out of the gate, still dancing and hopping until I felt far enough away from them.

As I ran away from Gath, I felt some of the greatest despair I had felt in a long time. I had gone to the only place I felt I could go for safety and I had failed. For a while I just ran without any direction at all. As I neared the border of Judah, I saw the mountains that had always been my home and decided to hide there. Despite the fact that it was not that far from Gibeah, I knew the mountains well and could move around easily if I needed to. Remembering a small cave that I had seen before on my trips in that area, I traveled to Adullam and hid there.

It wasn't long before my family came to the cave. I was so thankful that my father had the wisdom to speak with me when I was home during the festival. I needed their company so badly because I felt alone and discouraged. With the large number of us, we were able to set up a fairly good residence in the caves. We kept busy hunting and looking for food to feed us all. Despite my failures, Yahweh stayed near me, and I felt His presence during this lonely time. I sang again and wrote songs for Him. I rejoiced to be outside and with my loved ones again. At times, I almost forgot that Saul was out to kill me.

Yahweh, in His wisdom, sent others to join my group. He sent me some who were in trouble, others who were in debt, and many who were in desperate circumstances. So many people were feeling a lack of confidence in the king and through whispers here and there, knew they could find refuge in my band of warriors. I knew the king was still trying to find and kill me but I felt more confident in my ability to defend myself because I was surrounded with a band of about 400 people.

I took my parents to Moab to stay with the king there. I felt better about their safety away from the wilderness because they were now much older. It was still a job to manage such a large group of men, and I often worried about what we would do if Saul found us. How would I know if we needed to flee? Once again, I put my trust in Yahweh. I had seen the foolishness of my own decisions in my mess in Gath. I didn't want to make that mistake again.

Sometime after I returned from Moab, the prophet Gad came to our cave. I knew from the minute I saw him that he had bad news. "Yahweh sends a message that you should not stay in this fortress any longer. Leave now and go to the land of Judah." We packed up immediately, taking only the things we needed the most, and left for the forest of Hereth.

It was there that we got the horrible news. I will never forget that day. I was sitting in the middle of our camp when I saw a man running toward me through the trees. He looked wasted and terrified. I recognized him immediately. It was Abiathar, son of Ahimelech, the high priest. "He has killed them all, David, every single one. Only I have escaped." Then he threw himself down on the ground and wept.

I felt numb with pain and grief. As I listened to him, I knew it was my fault. I had not told Ahimelech the truth of why I had visited. I put his whole family in danger because of my foolishness. I knew when I saw Doeg there with Ahimelech that he would tell Saul everything. I knew ... and I said nothing. I screamed in anger at myself and sobbed in agony over what I had done. I told Abiathar I was sorry, but my words sounded so hollow compared to the magnitude of what just happened.

I felt numb with pain and grief. As I listened to him, I knew it was my fault.

We cried for a long time, and as the members of the band came by and heard the story, they wept also. The shock was overwhelming because no one believed that the king was capable of murdering the high priest, let alone all the priests. He blamed them because I had escaped the cave, and he ordered the deaths of Ahimelech's entire family. Doeg had done the violent deed, but the guilt was on the hands of the king. And on me.

I still can't shake the guilt I feel over the deaths of the priests. Abiathar gave me the ability to forgive myself for my foolish actions because he supported me and began to act as the high priest, testifying that Yahweh had chosen me to be the next king. It wasn't the kingship that I wanted, but the support of those who followed Yahweh and the knowledge that Yahweh accepted my cries of forgiveness helped me deal with my feelings. I knew I needed to depend on Him more, and I knew I needed the help of those around me to help me grow toward whatever He had planned for my future.

So once again I prayed and turned to my songwriting.

> O Lord, hear my plea for justice.
> Listen to my cry for help.
> Pay attention to my prayer,
> for it comes from honest lips.
> Declare me innocent,
> for you see those who do right.
> You have tested my thoughts and examined
> my heart in the night.
> I am praying to you because I know you will answer,
> O God.
> Bend down and listen as I pray.
> Show me your unfailing love in wonderful ways.
> By your mighty power you rescue
> those who seek refuge from their enemies.
> Guard me as you would guard your own eyes.
> Hide me in the shadow of your wings.[16]

---

[16] Psalm 17:1–3, 6–8.

CHAPTER 11

I have recently seen some things that I never would have believed could have happened if I had not lived through it myself. Yahweh has performed miracle after miracle for my salvation. I feel so undeserving of it, especially in light of my many mistakes. He is so faithful.

It began with a wonderful visit from Jonathan. Our little band was exhausted because we were always on the move. No matter where we went, it seemed Saul was on our path. We found ourselves camping out in the wilderness of Ziph when Jonathan entered our camp. His presence cheered my heart. We spoke, and he spent time with my men, who now numbered 600. Later in the evening, when we were alone, he asked me how we were doing. I was honest and told him that it had been a struggle and that we were exhausted. "Don't be afraid, David. My father won't touch you. You will be king over Israel someday, and I will be your second in command. Even my father knows that you are Yahweh's chosen."

I felt comforted by his words, not because he said I would be king, but because he wanted to be with me whether I was king or not. He understood my desire for friendship, and he renewed his covenant with me.

While he was still with us, a messenger came running into the camp. "The Ziphites have gone to the king and told him where you are. He is on his way with his army." We had only been there a short time, but we knew we couldn't linger. I hugged Jonathan goodbye, and we headed to the mountains between Maon and the Dead Sea.

We got word almost immediately at Maon that Saul was close behind. We were afraid. He had a large army with him, and we were big enough that we couldn't just hide behind a few trees. If he was anywhere near us, he would find us. Once again, I felt compelled to do something. But I could think of nothing. Feeling helpless, I turned to Yahweh. His gentle reminder that I should have done that at the beginning was exactly what I needed. I asked for forgiveness and committed myself to trusting in God.

I told my men that my own best efforts had always failed without Yahweh. No matter what came this time, we would let Him guide us out of this trap. So, we prayed together as Abiathar led us to seek God's face. He petitioned Yahweh for guidance, and then he began to walk. We followed. Sometimes his paths were straight and open. Sometimes they were jagged and strange. I know the men felt as though we were walking with no direction or purpose. I certainly did.

The hardest part of it was that we could hear Saul's army walking around in the same areas—always near us but never close enough to see us. We could hear their footsteps as if they were going to step right in front of us at any moment. But then they would move on to another area. This went on for what felt like forever, and then I heard them on the other side. Saul was raging.

"They are here! I feel and hear them! Why do we not find them?!" I peeked around the tree that blocked his view of me and could see that he was raging to Abner. "We will find them! They can't move around forever." From behind Saul, a messenger ran up panting. "Your majesty! You must come and bring the armies right away! The Philistines have invaded near Gibeah!" My heart about leaped out of my chest. Had Yahweh moved the Philistines on our behalf?

"Are you sure? We are so close!" Abner didn't move, but Saul had already begun signaling for the men to come in. "We will come again, Abner," he spoke wearily. "Next time you have to find him faster!" They were both angry with each other and most definitely with me. But I was so excited I could barely stay still while I waited for them to move on. Yahweh had just saved us without us doing anything—aside from trusting Him! He had performed a miracle that no one else could have done. I was trembling when I addressed my men. I passionately reminded them that Yahweh had delivered us! Then I began to sing a song I felt bubbling up inside of me. It wasn't finished, but I didn't care. I sang it loudly, and we danced and rejoiced.

> I will praise Your name, O Lord, for it is good.
> For you have rescued me from my troubles
> And helped me to triumph over my enemies.[17]

After this miracle, we moved on to the wilderness of En-gedi. I knew we were safe for a time, so we celebrated for a few more days, but I knew that the Ziphites would continue to give away our hiding places to Saul, so I continued to ask Yahweh for His guidance in every step we took. After refreshing ourselves in the springs around En-gedi, I went to a nearby cave to rest and talk to Yahweh.

We stayed in En-gedi for a while because it was a good place for us to find food, and the varied landscape allowed us to find some hiding places. We heard no word about the king for several days. Each day I spent time in the cave, enjoying the quiet moments talking to Yahweh. I would often take some of my closest warriors with me to the cave so that we could plan and strategize and talk. It was very important to me that they also be surrendered to Yahweh. If they were not supportive of allowing Him to lead us, it would be much harder to get everyone to follow.

---

[17] Psalm 54:6, 7.

Some days ago, we were resting in the cave when another miracle took place. We had been told by one of our scouts that Saul was in the area looking for us but that he had brought a group of men smaller than our numbers. Still exerting caution, we had the men scattered in various spots, hidden and watching. We had been doing this for about two days. It paid off. While we rested in the cave, we heard the sound of someone walking in. I stilled the men with a hand signal and we waited. Within a few seconds, we saw a man walk in. It was the king.

He was alone and appeared to be coming in to rest. We watched him in silence—our breathing almost nonexistent—as we waited to see what he would do. Walking without any concern that there might be people nearby, he found a spot near the side of the cave and laid down. Within less than a minute, we heard heavy breathing that quickly became a snore. The men stirred slightly, looking at each other and then at me. I didn't move.

Yahweh had just saved us without us doing anything—aside from trusting Him! He had performed a miracle that no one else could have done.

Finally, one of them slowly, with not a sound, moved to my side. "Yahweh promised that He would hand over your enemies to you. This is the day that His promise has come true." Pointing to the king, he continued speaking in as enthusiastic a voice as he could use without waking Saul. "Do with him whatever you want, General."

I looked in his direction. He lay so closely to us that I could reach him in two steps. If I killed him, he would never even know that it was me. Only the men in the cave would be witness, and not one of them would ever tell. My thoughts were all over the place. If I killed Saul, it would certainly make our lives easier. We would not always be leaving our families or running through the woods praying that it wasn't our last day. And the nation would be at peace. Wasn't this what Yahweh had in store when He said He would deliver my enemy to me?

The thoughts would have continued to increase in urgency except that one thought kept pushing the others to the side. It was really a voice that I heard loudly in my ear. "Do not touch those anointed by Yahweh." It was settled in my mind. I wouldn't do anything. I softly spoke to my men, reminding them that Yahweh forbid me to do anything to His anointed. Then, before they could argue or react, I moved swiftly and quietly to Saul's side and cut off a corner of his robe. I immediately felt horrible, like I was sick to my stomach. I crawled back to where my men sat in silence and put my head down on the ground, struggling to keep from vomiting.

I stayed there for a few minutes, and then I heard voices calling the king. He took a deep breath and stood up. Quickly brushing himself off, he grabbed his spear and went outside. I followed quickly but quietly, careful to stay behind him by about ten steps. He was deadly with his spear, and I didn't want to be in his throwing range. I stayed at the edge of the cave until he had walked all the way down the hill to the valley floor.

I then yelled down to the king. I waited for him to look up, and then I bowed to the ground. I didn't hear any movement, so I assumed he was frozen in place. I was still bowed low in respect. From my crouched position, I spoke these words, "Why do you listen to those who say that I am trying to ruin you? Look at me! Yahweh handed you to me in the cave, but I refused to kill you. I spared you saying that I would not lift a hand against Yahweh's anointed." Then I stood and held my arm up high with the piece of his robe fluttering in the breeze. "I am not guilty of wrongdoing or rebellion. Yet you are hunting me down to kill me. Am I a dog? Or a flea? May Yahweh judge us both for our actions. He may take vengeance on you, but I will not lift a hand against you." I lowered my arm and stood in silence, looking at him directly.

He spoke almost as soon as I finished, and his voice sounded odd. "David, my son, is that you?" He began to sob. "You are a better man than I am, for you have repaid me good for evil. Yes, you have been amazingly kind to me today, for when the Lord put me in a place where you could have killed me, you didn't do it. Who else would let his enemy get away when he had him in his power? May the Lord reward you well for the kindness you have shown me today."[18] He bowed his head for a moment and then lifted it and spoke with a softer voice. "And now I realize that you are surely going to be king, and that the kingdom of Israel will flourish under your rule. Now swear to me by the Lord that when that happens you will not kill my family and destroy my line of descendants!"[19]

I was moved by his words. I knew him to be a man I couldn't trust, but he spoke so compellingly—I wanted to believe everything he said. I made the pledge as he had requested, and then he left. He asked me to come back to the palace, but although I missed Michal and Jonathan and my home, I knew I could not fully trust Saul, and Yahweh reminded me that I had my men to protect as well. So, we stayed in the mountains and caves instead of moving back to the palace.

Not too long after my encounter with the king, we received word that the prophet Samuel had died. We were overcome with sadness and grief yet we knew he was peacefully resting. Yahweh's faithful servant had lived many years and done so much to draw the people to a better understanding of God. He had been Israel's leader before Saul ever became king. The nation mourned him as well. We all knew, however, that his death would mean the king had no positive influence at all and no one to remind him of his commitment to rule Yahweh's people. Under Yahweh's direction, we moved to the wilderness of Paran and hid from Saul again. It was a wise move because Saul quickly forgot our pledge and sought my life.

This time, when the king came to hunt us down, our spies warned us in advance. So, in the night, while the king and his soldiers slept in the wilderness, I took my nephew, Abishai, with me to see them. His camp was on Hakilah's hill near the road. We heard no sound and saw no motion

---

[18] 1 Samuel 24:17–19.
[19] 1 Samuel 24:20, 21.

from the camp, so we walked up quietly behind the trees and saw, right in front of us, the sleeping king. His spear was stuck in the ground by his head, along with a jug of water. General Abner lay next to him, snoring loudly. Not one soldier or spy or attendant seemed to be awake. I was amazed.

"Yahweh has handed your enemy to you today, David." Abishai excitedly said. "Let me pin him to the ground with my spear. I can do it in one stroke!" There was anger in his voice as he spoke. Although he was young, he knew the difficulties Saul had placed on our lives. This would be an easy solution.

He waited for my signal with his spear in his hands. It was tempting, but I knew the right answer. I told Abishai to lower his spear. I reminded him that Saul was still the Lord's anointed, and the Lord would have to be the One to strike him down. Yahweh had forbidden me to lift a hand against him, and I would obey. I looked at all the sleeping men, and then I instructed Abishai to take Saul's spear and water jug. Abishai walked softly and cautiously between the soldiers to the king's sleeping body and took the spear and jug. No one saw or knew we were there. They just slept. I am sure Yahweh put them into a deep sleep as He had done for Gideon when he fought the Midianites.

We left the camp and crossed to the other side of the hill. I wanted to be a good distance away before they woke. When we reached a place that was safe, and where they could see us, I shouted to Abner. At the sound of my voice, Abner and all the men jumped up, terrified. It took them some time to see us standing on the hill across the valley. "Who are you to shout to the king?" he yelled back at me.

There was a touch of sarcasm in my voice as I shouted back these words. "Abner, you are so mighty, a man with no equal in Israel. So why were you asleep when you should have been guarding the king? We could've killed him. You and your men deserve to die because you failed to protect the Lord' anointed. As proof of how close we were, look around you. Where are the king's spear and water jug, which were right beside his head?"

Maybe it was the humor in my voice or maybe it was the action of taking his things, but Saul recognized my voice. "David, my son, is that you?"

I told him it was indeed me, and then I asked him why he was chasing me, his servant no less. I asked him what I had done wrong to deserve such treatment. Then I suddenly felt as if this might be my last chance to say this, so I spoke these words with a sense of urgency in my voice. "Why are you chasing me? What have I done? What is my crime? But now let my lord the king listen to his servant. If the Lord has stirred you up against me, then let him accept my offering. But if this is simply a human scheme, then may those involved be cursed by the Lord. For they have driven me from my home, so I can no longer live among the Lord's people, and they have said, 'Go, worship pagan gods.' Must I die on foreign soil, far from the presence of the Lord? Why has the king of Israel come out to search for a single flea? Why does he hunt me down like a partridge on the mountains?"[20]

Saul's voice rung across the valley in agony. "I have sinned! Come back home, my son, and I will no longer try to harm you, for you valued my life today. I have been a fool and very, very wrong."[21] His voice chocked as he thought about what he had done. But this was all too reminiscent of our last encounter. I sighed. How I wished things could have been different. Despite his cries, I knew he would never change.

I asked for a servant to come and get his things, and he sent one. We said our goodbyes from across the valley, and he blessed me and left. As I returned to our hiding place, I knew that despite the king's promises, we had an uncertain future ahead of us. We were tired and ready to be done with this fugitive life. Yet, we had nowhere to go, and I had no idea what to do about it. I once again reached out to Yahweh. He had never failed us. I chose to praise Him despite my fear of the future. So, I sang a song with my men all around, knowing that we needed to praise Yahweh in the midst of our uncertainty and trust Him to guide us.

---

[20] 1 Samuel 26:18–20.
[21] 1 Samuel 26:21.

O God, you are my God;
I earnestly search for you.
My soul thirsts for you;
my whole body longs for you
in this parched and weary land
where there is no water.
I have seen you in your sanctuary
and gazed upon your power and glory.
Your unfailing love is better than life itself;
how I praise you!
I will praise you as long as I live,
lifting up my hands to you in prayer.
You satisfy me more than the richest feast.
I will praise you with songs of joy.[22]

---

[22] Psalm 63:1–5.

CHAPTER 12

Doubt is a strange and horrible thing. No matter how often I try to avoid it, it just sits there waiting for me. It seems to understand that if it waits long enough I will eventually give in. I am sad to say that I have given in many times.

After the second time I refused to take the life of the king, I found that despite the time I spent talking to Yahweh and waiting for his leading, I still doubted His guidance for the future. The more I thought about Saul, the more I couldn't shake the idea that he would keep coming for me. I had 600 men, but every one of them was worn down from always hiding and running. I knew Saul would come again. I knew we'd have another interaction just like the previous ones. There was no way that we could keep surviving the way we had.

So, I gave in. Rather than trust that Yahweh would continue to provide a way until He brought about His plan, I made a choice that I felt would help us out of the situation we were in. I took my men to Gath, hoping we could escape Saul and talk Achish into allowing us to fight for him. I don't know what I was thinking, since the last time I attempted this plan I ended up drooling all over myself just to get out alive. But this time I was taking 600 men with me, so I felt more protected.

When I met with Achish, I asked for a town that he could give us so that we could house our families and the other people in our band. He was agreeable to the whole set up and gave us the town of Ziklag. I'm sure he needed soldiers, and thinking about it now, I am sure he was thinking we'd fight against Israel with him. He probably reasoned that since I had left Israel, I must have something against them and being a fugitive would have no problem fighting against my own.

Ziklag was in the south, so we were responsible for raiding the southern part of his territory. We did this on a regular basis and established ourselves nicely in Ziklag. Ignoring the fact that I had been anointed by Yahweh to defend His chosen people, I assumed that since we were out of the way, doing our own thing, my decision to join the Philistines had been a good one. But then Achish called on us to represent Gath in a battle against the Israelites. He had told me that he was counting on us to help him fight, and I had agreed, not sure how I would get myself out of the trouble I was now facing.

When it was time for the Philistine cities to bring their forces together, we showed up. We had to. My men were unhappy about it, as was I, but I held true to my word. There were others besides us, though, that were also unhappy with the arrangement. The other Philistine commanders didn't like us being there.

"Who are the Hebrews?" asked one of the commanders angrily. "It's David," replied Achish proudly. "He's a servant of King Saul. He's been fighting with me for a year. There's nothing wrong with him. He's been an asset since the day he arrived."

It didn't matter what he said. As soon as they heard my name, they were in an uproar. "Send him home, Achish! He cannot go to battle with us. Couldn't he just turn against us in the middle of the fight? What a great idea it would be for him if he wanted to please his master, the king! Have you forgotten, Achish? This is the one who has killed his tens of thousands."

So Achish sent us home. I acted insulted that we couldn't fight, but when we got far enough away from Gath, we were all extremely thankful. I felt even more grateful to Yahweh because, I had put us in this position without Yahweh's permission, and now He had bailed me out. My choices had led us to the point that we would have been fighting against our own king and relatives. I was horrified by the thought that I or one of my men might have faced Jonathan on the battlefield. Yahweh, in His mercy, had pulled us out of the trap in which I had put us. I said many prayers of thanks on our journey back to Ziklag.

It took us about three days to travel each way between Gath and Ziklag because Gath was the northernmost city in Philistia, and Ziklag was the southernmost area that Gath controlled. I will never forget the shock and horror we all felt as we reached the top of the hill where we gained our first view of the city—it was desolate.

We ran in terror toward the city, noticing along the way that it had been burned almost to nothing. Anything of worth or value was gone.

We ran in terror toward the city, noticing along the way that it had been burned almost to nothing. Anything of worth or value was gone, and the walls that were left standing were black and crumbling, barely hanging together in the piles of ashes all around. For a few minutes we all stood at the entrance to the town and stared at it in silence. Every eye moved across the scene, looking for some sign that our loved ones were alive. The town itself didn't matter. We just hoped that our families might come walking out from behind some pile of rubble. But there was nothing. Not one person was there.

Rage, anger, agony, and extreme sorrow overtook us and we wept bitterly. Every one of my 600 men had lost someone, and we wailed loudly in grief. We cried for a long time. Then the grief turned to anger, which was all directed at me.

My men's rage increased, and some of the soldiers shouted that I should be stoned. It caught momentum, and the number who agreed increased. My own men were turning on me! I fervently prayed a song that I had written.

> Have compassion on me, Lord,
> For I am weak.
> Heal me, Lord,
> For my bones are in agony!
> I am sick at heart.
> How long, O Lord, until you restore me?
> Return, O Lord, and rescue me.
> Save me because of your unfailing love.[23]

    While I prayed, several of the men who had begun to look around the city, ran back to the group of men surrounding me and said. "Hold tight! This is the work of the Amalekites!" Everyone stopped and turned to listen. "Look!" The group showed us a pile of Amalekite clothing items and weapon pieces that confirmed the truth. The Amalekites, angry at us for raiding them, had come to seek revenge. We had raided the Amalekites to keep Achish happy, and now it had come back to haunt me. Angry voices rose again.

    "But wait!" One of my closest fighters stepped up. "There is also evidence that the Amalekites have taken our women and children alive to celebrate the victory when they return home. Look at the tracks leading out of the city." We stepped to the side and noticed a handful of footprints among the ashes. "This didn't happen too long ago. If it had, the footprints would have been blown away by the wind. They have taken our families, and if we are fast, we can catch them before they get to Amalek." Voices began to simmer and argue and debate. He interrupted with a sense of urgency. "The longer we spend discussing and debating, the closer our families are to slavery or death. What are we waiting for?"

---

[23] Psalm 6:2–4.

I stepped forward and took the blame for the tragedy that had befallen us. I acknowledged before the men that I had not sought Yahweh's guidance for my decisions, which had gotten us into trouble. I told them that we could not make the same mistake and that we needed to ask Yahweh what we should do before chasing after the Amalekites. Abiathar the high priest stepped forward and began to seek God's guidance.

Yahweh's answer came back strong and definitive. "Go after them! You will catch them and succeed in rescuing your families." I don't think we waited more than a second before we began to run. Every one of the 600 men was inspired and energized to rescue their loved ones. We kept up the blistering fast pace for a few hours until we reached the Besor ravine. We had been moving so quickly that many of the men were straggling and not able to continue without resting. Two hundred of them stayed at the ravine to rest. I pushed on with the rest.

Not too long after leaving the ravine, we found an Egyptian slave who had been left to die. He was unable to move or speak because he was so hungry and thirsty. Knowing that it was not right to leave him dying, and hoping that he had been with the Amalekites, we pulled him to some shade and gave him some bread and water. Then, my nephew Abishai pulled some fig and raisin cakes that he had in his pouch. As the Egyptian ate, he seemed to regain his strength. The water also helped immensely. As he revived, he told us that he hadn't eaten or had any water for three days and nights. He would have died without us.

As soon as he was able to talk, I asked him whose slave he was and where he had come from. "I'm Egyptian, and my master is an Amalekite. He abandoned me when I got sick three days ago." He was young and earnest when he spoke, and he looked at me with intensity in his eyes, despite his weakness. "We raided the arid southern plain belonging to the Cherethites, the territory belonging to Judah, and the southern plain of Caleb. We also burned down Ziklag." I bristled and looked carefully at the men around me, watching to make sure that none would attack the boy.

I asked him if he could lead us to the raiding party. I watched to see if he would respond positively. "Promise me that you won't kill me or hand me over to my master." He looked directly at me with the same intensity. "If you promise, I will guide you to them." I agreed.

We heard the noise of the celebration coming from the camp before we saw anything or anyone. They were scattered all over the area where they had set up camp. Everywhere we looked, we could see them eating or drinking, dancing or slumped over in a stupor of drunkenness. It was clear that they had been celebrating their plunder. My anger raged. I wanted to move in and take them out immediately. It would be dark soon, so I made a loud shout and ran straight for them, knowing my men would react in the same way. They did.

All four hundred of us attacked immediately. We naturally surprised them, which threw them into a state of confusion. We fought through the night and the next day, killing almost every single one of them. The only ones who escaped were a group of about 400 young men who jumped on camels and ran off.

The most amazing part was that we rescued every single thing they had taken, including our families. Not one thing that had been ours was missing. And we found every one of our family members. We brought everything back. We also took all the sheep and cattle that they had with them, rejoicing at our victory.

On our way home we met up with the 200 soldiers who had stayed at the ravine to rest and recover. They greeted us joyfully, happy to see their loved ones. There were some in our group, though, who were not happy to see them. "We aren't sharing any of the plunder we rescued because you didn't go with us! You can have your families back but that's it!" I was upset. I reminded them that this was Yahweh's victory, not ours. He had given us everything back. This was ultimately His plunder, so we would split it equally among everyone.

I let them know that we would continue with that method from that moment forward. We also shared some of the plunder with other inhabitants of Judah who had been affected by the raiders. I knew with certainty that Yahweh alone kept our families safe. His restraining power had kept the Amalekites from killing them all, which would have been much easier. Despite our mistakes, particularly mine, He worked on our behalf to keep our families safe and allow us to rescue them. We celebrated the wonder of our God as we returned home.

We had much to do in Ziklag to repair it and make it livable again, so we immediately began work on the city. Although we had a lot to keep our minds busy, we were distracted by the battle we knew was raging between the Philistines and the Israelites up north. We had not forgotten that we were supposed to be in the thick of the battle. We waited anxiously for news to reach us. The third day after our arrival back home, a messenger staggered up to the place where I was working in the city.

His clothes were torn and dirty, and he had dirt all over his head. When he walked up to me, he fell to the ground and bowed. My heart was pounding. "I've escaped from the Israelite army! The troops fled from the battle! Many of the soldiers have fallen and died. What's more, Saul and his son Jonathan have also died!" Fear grabbed me, and I stared at him in horror. I asked him how he could be sure that they were both dead.

"I just happened to be on the Mount Gilboa and Saul was there, leaning on his spear, with chariots and horsemen closing in on him. He turned around and saw me, then he called to me. He asked me to come over to him and kill him because convulsions had come over him and he was still alive. So, I did as he asked because I knew he would not survive. I took the crown from his head and his bracelet and have brought them to you, master." He held them out to me and then placed them at my feet. I could tell from his face that he expected an award of some kind, perhaps even a position of status. Instead, I cried out loudly.

I ripped my clothes in agony, and my men did the same, crying and mourning the loss of our king. We fasted and cried the whole day. Then I sang a funeral song for them.

> Your pride and joy, O Israel, lies dead on the hills!
> Oh, how the mighty heroes have fallen!
> O mountains of Gilboa,
> Let there be no dew or rain upon you,
> Nor fruitful fields producing offerings of grain.
> For there the shield of the mighty heroes was defiled;
> The shield of Saul will no longer be anointed with oil.
> How beloved and gracious were Saul and Jonathan!
> They were together in life and in death.
> They were swifter than eagles, stronger than lions.
> Oh, how the mighty heroes have fallen in battle!
> Jonathan lies dead on the hills.
> How I weep for you, my brother Jonathan!
> Oh, how much I loved you![24]

I knew that everyone was agonizing over the loss of the king and Jonathan. I knew I wasn't the only one mourning. I wanted to make sure, for myself most of all, but for each person in our group, that we remembered that despite our grief Yahweh was in control and that He mourned their deaths with us. So, I finished with a song for Him.

> O God, listen to my cry!
> Hear my prayer!
> From the ends of the earth,
> I cry to you for help when my heart is overwhelmed.
> Lead me to the towering rock of safety,
> For you are my safe refuge,
> A fortress where my enemies cannot reach me.
> Let me live forever in your sanctuary,
> Safe beneath the shelter of your wings![25]

---

[24] 2 Samuel 1:19–26.
[25] Psalm 61:1–4.

CHAPTER 13

We spent many days mourning the death of Saul and Jonathan. While it removed the danger from my life, I couldn't celebrate. Instead, I waited for instructions from Yahweh. Finally, after a long time, I asked Him if I should go to one of the towns in Judah. He told me to go to Hebron.

So, I took my family and my men in a large caravan up the road to Hebron. As we entered the city, the men of Judah welcomed me as king and made arrangements for a coronation.

When the time came, the people joined and celebrated as I was anointed their king. I honored those who had taken care of Saul and his sons after their deaths, and I honored those who were there. Most of all, I honored Yahweh in song.

>Yahweh, how majestic is Your name!
>When I look at the night sky,
>I see the works of your fingers.
>The moon and the stars
>Are set firmly in place

> What are we, mere mortals, that you should think about us?
> What are we, mere humans, that you should care about us?
> Yahweh, how majestic is Your name!
> We will thank You with all our hearts;
> We will talk about all Your wonderful acts.
> We will celebrate and rejoice in You;
> We will sing praises to Your name, Most High.[26]

It was a wonderful celebration of Yahweh and His work in my life and the lives of my people. As I sit here writing this entry in my journal, I am amazed at all He has done for me and for this nation. It took some time for all of Israel to accept me as king. There were many hardships and struggles and sad moments. But just as Yahweh promised so very long ago, through Samuel, I am now king of all Israel.

> *I don't fully understand His ways, and I certainly don't know the future. But I know that He is forever merciful and forever just and forever loving.*

I marvel at the fact that He picked someone like me, because I am not built like a king as Saul was. I am also not from a family with any kind of status. Even my home and my tribe in the south can be looked upon with criticism. But more than that, I can recount all of the mistakes I have made from childhood until now. I have forgotten Yahweh many times even when I committed to seek His guidance at all times. I have made poor choices that risked the lives of others who were so valuable to me. I am not worthy or deserving of the honor He has given me. And yet, here I am, His king.

I don't fully understand His ways, and I certainly don't know the future. But I know that He is forever merciful and forever just and forever loving. No matter what He chooses for me, I want it. No matter where He asks me to go, I want to follow. I have seen and felt what it means to make

---

[26] Based on Psalm 8 and 9.

decisions without Him, and it's not good. I am happy only when I let Him lead. He knows me, He loves me, He is my God, and I am His.

> O Lord, you have examined my heart
> and know everything about me.
> You know when I sit down or stand up.
> You know my thoughts even when I'm far away.
> You go before me and follow me.
> You place your hand of blessing on my head.
> You made all the delicate, inner parts of my body
> and knit me together in my mother's womb.
> Thank you for making me so wonderfully complex!
> Your workmanship is marvelous—how well I know it.[27]
> Create in me a clean heart, O God.
> Renew a loyal spirit within me.
> Do not banish me from your presence,
> and don't take your Holy Spirit[d] from me.
> Restore to me the joy of your salvation,
> and make me willing to obey you.[28]

My name is David, and I am king of Israel. I serve Yahweh and will serve Him all my days because He is my God and He is worthy. May my heart forever be like His.

---

[27] Psalm 139:1, 2, 5, 13, 14.
[28] Psalm 51:10–12.

TEACH Services, Inc.
P U B L I S H I N G
www.TEACHServices.com • (800) 367-1844

We invite you to view the complete
selection of titles we publish at:
www.TEACHServices.com

We encourage you to write us
with your thoughts about this,
or any other book we publish at:
info@TEACHServices.com

TEACH Services' titles may be purchased in
bulk quantities for educational, fund-raising,
business, or promotional use.
bulksales@TEACHServices.com

Finally, if you are interested in seeing
your own book in print, please contact us at:
publishing@TEACHServices.com
We are happy to review your manuscript at no charge.

www.ingramcontent.com/pod-product-compliance
Lightning Source LLC
Chambersburg PA
CBHW070543170426
43200CB00011B/2535